Human Rights in a Big Yellow Taxi

by Peter Kerr

Vagabond Voices
Glasgow

© Peter Kerr September 2013

First published in September 2013 by
Vagabond Voices Publishing Ltd.,
Glasgow,
Scotland.

ISBN 978-1-908251-17-6

The author's right to be identified as author of this book under the Copyright, Designs and Patents Act 1988 has been asserted.

Printed and bound in Poland

Cover design by Mark Mechan

Typeset by Park Productions

The publisher acknowledges subsidy towards this publication from Creative Scotland

For further information on Vagabond Voices, see the website, www.vagabondvoices.co.uk

For Marilyn

Contents

1. The Case of Power vs the People 1
2. Common Law 16
3. The Rule of Law 21
4. Human Rights 42
5. Freedom and Rights 55
6. Positive Freedom 87
7. Rights 91
8. Conclusion 107

Human Rights in a Big Yellow Taxi

The Case of Power vs the People

It was reported in the *Guardian* newspaper on Friday 10th December 2010 that a twelve-year-old schoolboy in Eynsham, Oxfordshire, was taken out of a class during school time and questioned by anti-terrorist police for trying to organise a protest picket outside the constituency office of the British Prime Minister David Cameron, who was also the MP for that constituency. The purpose of this picket was to protest at the threatened closure of the youth centre the young boy attended as a result of the Cameron government's budget cuts. An estimated 130 other children who use youth centres throughout the Prime Minister's constituency had been attracted to the idea through the Facebook website. During the interview with the police officer from Thames Valley police, the young boy, Nicky, was told that, if any public disorder took place outside the Cameron constituency office, he would be held responsible and would be arrested. He was then told that, even if he was not present during the disorder, he would still be held responsible and arrested. However, the officer then proceeded to tell this twelve-year-old boy that if the Prime Minister was in his office at the time, there would be armed officers in attendance. The officer then told the boy, "so if anything out of line happens…" he stopped there and didn't elaborate any further. This interview took place in the formal setting of the school and in the presence of another adult in a position of authority, the boy's head of year, but not in the presence of his parents. That this action terrified this young boy goes without saying. To most logical and intelligent people living in the modern setting of what we call a liberal democracy and a free society, such as the United Kingdom, terrorising a boy with threats of arrest and unspoken threats of being shot by armed police through the medium of the anti-terrorist branch of the police force in a formal setting flanked with authority figures identifies a terrorist state. In addition, most logical and intelligent people would ask themselves why the police were monitoring a twelve-year-old boy's Facebook website in the first place? When situations like this arise within our nation, it is time for the citizens of the United Kingdom to pause and consider the political environment that now prevails in the UK that produces the type of police officer who would do such a thing as threaten a twelve-year-old boy with arrest and the possibility of being shot, and would obey an order from a superior officer to do such a thing in any circumstances. This is particularly relevant when the young boy is merely exercising a right, the right of peaceful protest that extends back to Magna Charta. Surely any normal intelligent human being, whether they are a police officer or not, would simply refuse to obey such an instruction? However, much more importantly, what kind of authority structure now prevails within our police forces that would order officers to not only monitor such websites, but order such action to be taken?

But of particular significance to all people in the UK is the question of what type of political mentality motivates any MP, let alone the Prime Minister, to sanction such an action? What on earth was Cameron afraid of from a twelve-year-old boy that he sent the anti-terrorist branch of the police to silence him and prevent his small, but perfectly legitimate, protest? I mean, these things just don't happen in Britain, do they? We protect our children; we don't threaten them with the might of the state, do we? Such an action would be shocking if it was taken against any citizen of the United Kingdom, but to visit this on a twelve-year-old schoolchild defies intelligent understanding. Incidentally, serious questions must be asked about the head teacher of the boy's school who allowed the police to conduct themselves like that on school premises, particularly in the absence of the child's parents. In such circumstances that head teacher is responsible for the health and safety of all the pupils in his/her care and is responsible to the child and his parents, not to the police. What is happening to authority in the UK? Indeed, what is the nature of authority in modern Britain? What it does tend to suggest is that the "authorities" in the UK are losing their authority in the eyes of the public and are having to resort to raw power to achieve their objectives. That's what happens in any social organisation, when the leaders fail to lead and fail to have the authority of their office recognised as legitimate; they resort to bullying, to raw power. Make no mistake; what those police (supported by a Prime Minister and the police and education authorities) did is outright bullying. Bullying is the response of the weak and cowardly. It is also the response of the incompetent. Bullying is one of the chief characteristics of modern Britain. It runs like a cancer throughout the whole society and in all organisations and institutions. Strong competent leaders, managers etc. have no need to bully. People recognise the strong and the competent and respect them. They also respect their authority. The competent manager has no need to bully. He/she leads by example, and subordinates follow and respect such examples. As a result, it is vital that we question and challenge occurrences such as those described above, and ask ourselves what they tell about the nature of the state and politics in modern Britain? These types of behaviour by the agencies of the state are a clear sign of an increasing authoritarianism that is unfortunately gathering momentum. One of the things it definitely suggests is, that from the perspective of the authorities in Britain, from the Prime Minister to the forces of law and order and officials at all levels, terrorism means any challenge to the system, the law, or any aspect of the status quo, whether by peaceful or legal means, or not. The dominant ideological, legal, economic or political system must not be challenged and any challenge will be deemed terrorist.

The 1998 Human Rights Act was a measure passed by the UK Parliament expressly for the purpose of allowing British judges to implement the rulings of the European Court of Human Rights in British courts. Since then twenty-five Acts of Parliament and fifty individual measures have been passed at this time of writing removing rights that were established in the Human Rights Act, as well as others that have been rights for British citizens since Magna Carta. Throughout this time sections of the British elite and their supporters in the media have sustained a campaign of denigration and open hostility to the European Court of Human Rights on the grounds that the Court infringes the sovereignty of Parliament. This is of course nonsense, as the 1998 Act was a deliberative decision of a sovereign parliament to embrace the philosophy and decision-making of the European Court. In addition, the British Parliament has a representative on the bench of the European Court, and is therefore involved in all decisions emanating from that Court. The problem is that the Court sometimes passes measures and makes rulings that the British don't like and so they take the huff when they don't get their own way – and in the UK the elite must get their own way. This highlights a serious malaise at the heart of British government: the attempt to enshrine a standard of human rights and legal protections for the British people whilst at the same time actively removing rights, some of which are centuries old, and attacking the European Court responsible for maintaining and sustaining the rights you have just agreed to uphold in an Act of Parliament. There is only one conclusion you can draw from Britain's behaviour: the 1998 Act was a public relations exercise that Parliament had no intention of taking seriously. There is thus a serious cause for concern in the behaviour of the British government, as this is neither sane nor rational behaviour, and results in the anti-terrorist branch of the police force monitoring children's websites and terrorising them at their school. However, there is a demonstrable reason for such behaviour, and it is because British governments, since the election of Margaret Thatcher, have been zealous advocates of a free market neo-liberal economic theory that sees human rights as an economic cost, in addition to imposing political constraints on governments who now believe that being elected gives them the absolute right to do whatever they wish, whenever they wish to do it, whilst being totally unaccountable to anyone, particularly the electorate. Workers' rights, for example, are a constraint on employers, and the neo-liberal cannot tolerate constraints on employers and the pursuit of profit. As a result, workers' rights have been savagely attacked in a series of anti-union Acts of Parliament. Protests, regardless of their aims or the issues they are highlighting, are condemned for causing disruption and the police are allowed to act in whatever way they see fit to prevent such disruption. At the time of writing a debate is being conducted in the UK as to whether the police should be allowed to shoot demonstrators, and a group of eminent scientists has issued a warning that the government are planning to allow the police to use nerve gas against protestors. It was reported in the *Independent* newspaper on 7 February 2012 that:

> A high-level group of experts has asked the Government to clarify its position on whether it intends to develop "incapacitating chemical agents" for a range of domestic uses that go beyond the limited use of chemical irritants such as CS gas for riot control.
>
> The experts were commissioned by the Royal Society, the UK's national academy of sciences, to investigate new developments in neuroscience that could be of use to the military. They concluded that the Government may be preparing to exploit a loophole in the Chemical Weapons Convention allowing the use of incapacitating chemical agents for domestic law enforcement.

Can any reasonable person born into and brought up in the United Kingdom imagine any government actually considering such a proposal? It seems like the plot of a bad Hollywood movie! Such things just don't happen in the UK, do they? So why are they? Well they are happening because of Britain's commitment to free market neo-liberal economic theory, to the political and social imperatives required by neo-liberal reality, and to the determination of the authorities that implementation of free market policies will neither be challenged nor obstructed. To the neo-liberal free market mindset, anything that affects economic considerations and the endless pursuit of profits is bad; and considerations of human welfare and political rights are unimportant and a nuisance. For Tony Blair human rights were a constraint on his "war on terror", which involved the bombing and invasion of other countries and the torture and "rendition" (neo-liberal jargon for kidnapping) of people in the pursuit of oil revenues. Blair desired to incarcerate people indefinitely without charge and without trial or access to legal representation. To achieve his aims he shamelessly lied to Parliament and the British people, and was supported by a craven set of supporters in his governments, in the press and by civil servants, who all knew that what they were telling the people was pure fiction. In such matters, Blair and his governments were simply following the lead of the United States, of whom Blair's New Labour Party were slavish admirers. In this Blair was supported uncritically by the Conservatives who would remove all rights from people who are even mildly critical of them and their policies and who would happily deliver the United Kingdom up as a provincial government of the United States. As a result, we should take great notice of what the Americans do in such matters, because what America does today, the British government will do tomorrow.

On 31 December 2011 the President of the United States, Barack Obama, signed into law the National Defense Authorization Act (NDAA) for Fiscal Year 2012. This law gives explicit authority to the US military to seize any person they please, anywhere in the world, including US citizens, and detain them indefinitely without charge, without trial, without access to legal representation or their family, in short without any rights whatsoever. This Act is in direct contravention of the American Constitution (Sixth Amendment: the right to seek legal counsel) and what Americans call the Miranda process (being informed of your rights when arrested). In October 2011, the news agency Reuters reported that American citizens accused of any form of involvement in terrorism can be "placed on a kill or capture list by a secretive panel of senior government officials, which then informs the president of its decisions ... There is no public record of the operations or decisions of the panel ... Neither is there any law establishing its existence or setting out the rules by which it is supposed to operate." What is significant about this is that there is no process of law involved. The people responsible for ordering the imprisonment or murder of American citizens are not legal officers but officials appointed by the government and working without any obvious rules or legal guidance, and the people responsible for the seizure and abduction of people throughout the world are the military. Would any other country be authorised to capture its citizens anywhere in the world and detain them without charge or trial or access to family or legal representation indefinitely? Our experience would suggest that the United States would immediately go to war if its own citizens were treated in this manner. Can you also imagine what the response of the Americans would be if any other country placed its citizens on a kill or capture list without the due process of law, or any involvement by the law enforcement agencies of that country? They would cry, "Fascism". They would brand that country tyrannical. In March 2012, President Obama signed into law a measure that is known as HR 347 which is the "Federal Restricted Buildings and Grounds Improvement Act of 2011". The HR, in HR 347, stands for the House of Representatives and its twin measure passing through the Senate was S. 1974. This measure provides the authorities with the ability to designate any form of protest a federal offence carrying a penalty of one to ten years in federal prison if the protest takes place in the presence of any designated elite who qualify for secret service protection, or, during any event that is officially defined as a "National Security Special Event" (NSSE). NSSEs are events that are considered worthy of secret service protection. Events that have merited this designation by the authorities in recent years have been the funerals of Gerald Ford and Ronald Reagan, Superbowl XXXV1, the Academy Awards presentations and the Democratic and Republican conventions. This measure appears to contradict American law and Supreme Court rulings. For example, in 1989, in a case known as *Texas* v *Johnson*, a protest was held outside the Republican National Convention being held in Dallas, Texas, in the course of which a man called Johnson burned an American flag. In Texan law, the desecration of the flags of Texas and the United States is a criminal offence and Johnson was arrested, fined 2000 dollars and sentenced to one year in jail. However, Johnson's sentence was overturned by both the Supreme Courts of Texas and the United States, on the grounds that this form of self-expression was protected under the First Amendment to the US Constitution. The US Supreme Court stated that flag burning was "expressive conduct" because it attempted to "convey a particularised message". The concept of NSSEs did not exist prior to 1998 when President Clinton created them as part of "Presidential Decision

Directive 62". As a result, an American President can, on a whim, criminalise any form of protest they consider to be inconvenient or embarrassing. I am not an American, but it would appear to me that President Obama has just outlawed a form of political activity that was ruled constitutionally legal by the Supreme Court in 1989. In another blow to personal freedom, the US Supreme Court ruled, on Monday 2 April 2012, that the US prison service is not guilty of violating the rights of personal privacy by the practice of strip-searching every person arrested no matter what the offence, even minor offences such as traffic violations. The Court ruled that such searches outweighed concerns for privacy rights on the grounds of security where jails had concerns about suspects hiding drugs, weapons or other contraband material. Stripping someone naked in the presence of other people is the first step in a process of dehumanising and has been recognised as such for centuries. That is what the Nazis did to prisoners entering the concentration camps. Americans should be deeply worried about the creeping authoritarianism of their government.

In January 2012, the British government, under an initiative from the Justice Secretary Ken Clarke, were preparing to remove a human rights guarantee that was introduced in Magna Charta in 1215 in clause 40: "To no one will we sell, to no one deny or delay right or justice." This is a clause embodying what we call common law, and Clarke was planning to introduce a clause into law that would allow any minister to suppress any information, and forbid it to be introduced into court if he/she considers it to be "sensitive" or "against the public interest". Under this proposal, material that would reveal the government's involvement in the torture or rendition of alleged terrorists would not be admitted in evidence. Importantly, this clause will also cover any material that a minister claims is sensitive or against the public interest, such as police corruption, ministers involved in criminality, leaks in nuclear reactors etc., in short, anything that may embarrass the authorities. Quite astonishingly Clarke stated on national television that this action was necessary because the Americans wanted it. As the *Guardian's* legal correspondent, Joshua Rozenberg reported on Wednesday April 4 2012, in response to its examination of Clarke's proposals, the UK Parliament's Joint Committee on Human Rights noted that the proposals, contained in a green paper, were designed to reassure the Americans that their intelligence would not be shared against the British government's wishes (a green paper is a publication by the government on specific detailed issues that points the way towards possible courses of action, and is a preliminary step in preparing a new piece of legislation. The Oxford English Dictionary describes it as "a preliminary report of government proposals published to stimulate discussion"). The Americans were concerned over evidence being disclosed regarding the incarceration of a British citizen, Binyam Mohamed, in Guantanamo Bay prison. This case involved allegations of torture by the American authorities, and complicity in that torture by the British, including the government. This admission by the British government that British legal processes were being devised to please a foreign government, and protect the British authorities from involvement in illegal acts, must demonstrate once and for all that we are in thrall to the Americans. This measure, if enacted into law, will effectively place government and its agencies above the law, simply by allowing a minister to declare any material sensitive or against public (or American) interest. Thus, any British citizen can be denied "right or justice" and have their rights to justice delayed indefinitely and indeed completely suppressed. What we must highlight here is that in such legal matters, it is not, and must never be, within the remit of any politician to determine what is or is not in the public interest. That should be a matter for the courts to decide, and anyway, what right has any politician who is elected by the public, paid by the public, and accountable to the public, to decide what is or is not in their interest, particularly when it involves the arrest and imprisonment, often without charge, of our fellow citizens? If it happens to one, it can then happen to anyone, and for reasons that the government will refuse to disclose. The public, like ignorant children, are supposedly incapable of handling certain information. There may be a case for withholding certain forms of legal information from general release, but such decisions should only be taken by tried and tested procedures and processes that the public can have some measure of confidence in. We should be very alarmed when any politician interferes with the traditions of our common law.

Common Law

Common law is the principle of establishing legal decisions on precedent rather than simply relying on statutory law and legislative enactments. If there is a particular statute applicable to the case under consideration, then a determination will be made by judicial interpretation of the relevant statute in accordance with decisions that have been reached by previous historical judicial precedent. In other words, common law relies on accumulated wisdom and agreed legal practice over the historical experience of the British legal system. Common law is founded on decisions that have successfully settled legal controversies, and judges will consult previous cases and reports on decisions that have successfully determined such previous controversies, rather than a reliance on the letter of the law in any particular legal code or text. In other words, common law is empirical; it relies on legal precedent and experience. In the British legal system there is a principle known as *stare decisis* ("to stand by that which is decided") which requires the judiciary to respect and be guided by previously decided cases, what we have called precedents, where the facts are substantially the same. This gives continuity to the law, and ensures a measure of justice. The accumulated experience of such historical decisions is held to be reliable and just, thereby giving authority to the judges deciding the case before them. A particular strength of common law is that it allows for flexibility when dealing with modern developments for which there are no precedents. As social change occurs all the time, and in a modern world with increasing rapidity, the judiciary is often faced with situations where there are no precedents. Such situations are known as "cases of first impression". The principles of common law allow the judiciary to draw on past and present experience of *similar* cases or principles, and also to look to other areas of the law to provide guidance in such circumstances. Utilising the principle of *stare decisis*, the judiciary are able to draw on a tradition and principle that will help them in uncharted territory to reach decisions that accord with the need for the stability and uniformity required in a functional and just legal system. However, perhaps most importantly for this discussion, under our system of common law justice, cases are settled by the adversarial methodology of legal argument and evidence. Arguments for and against are placed before a neutral referee, either a judge or a jury, who are required to evaluate the evidence, apply the relevant law, and reach a judgement. If this judgement is considered unsatisfactory by any of the parties in the case, they have the right of appeal. Equally important is the concept that under common law, all citizens are both equal before the law, and subject to it. This includes all government personnel and officials, whose power is limited and constrained by the law. Common law is not only a reflection of the accumulated legal wisdom of years of practice and application – it is also a reflection of the nation's culture, its norms and values. It must not be dismissed lightly, and certainly should not be ignored. It is a safeguard against arbitrary power and essential to the rule of law. It belongs to the people and must not be considered the gift or whim of governments that come and go.

Ken Clarke's proposal follows the quite extraordinary move by the New Labour government under its Special Immigration Appeals Commission which introduced what Labour termed its "closed material procedure". This mechanism allowed evidence to be withheld from an individual and that individual's legal team. The evidence is presented to an appointed "special advocate" who is tasked with protecting the individual's interests. However, this special advocate is also denied any contact with either the individual he/she is supposed to be representing or with their legal team as well. So, the special advocate is only presented with the government's case and has no way to check or verify the details with the person or persons involved. To any rational person this seems quite hard to believe, that a so-called democratic nation claiming to be governed by the rule of law would conduct itself in such a patently unlawful and unjust manner. One of the oldest maxims in law is the principle that justice must not only be done, but must be seen to be done. Giving the Atkin Memorial Lecture in 2011, Dinah Rose, a leading British Queen's Counsel, commented that this legislation would "permit courts to try common law claims for damages using a closed material procedure, whenever a government minister, who is, of course, likely to be party to the action, decides that disclosure of particular material would be damaging to national security". She likened the process for a lawyer involved in such a case to that of being asked to shoot blindly at a concealed target. Whether the measure proposed by Clarke becomes law or not, from our point of view the fact that it has even been proposed is a matter of great concern. Labour has already implemented the principle of denying rights and justice and Clarke's measure will consolidate and deepen this governmental crime. Make no mistake, this is state criminality and a negation of the rule of law. The willingness of government and its ministers to propose such reforms demonstrates the rot and corruption in governmental and legal processes in modern Britain. These measures can only be designed to protect torturers and criminals who are acting on behalf of the authorities, and to allow the state and its agencies at all levels of society to subvert and avoid the due process of law. As we noted, both the United States and Britain are acting in direct contradiction to their own constitutional and common law traditions. To quote St Augustine of Hippo: "Surely we will not dare say that these laws are unjust, or rather, that they are not laws at all. For it seems to me that an unjust law is no law at all." St Thomas Aquinas argued that we cannot be bound to obey laws that are manifestly unjust because laws that violate reason are not laws, they are something else, and Supreme Court Justice Louis Brandeis stated in 1928, "If the government becomes a law-breaker, it breeds contempt for the law. It invites every man to become a law unto himself. It invites anarchy." As early as 1686 Sir Robert Atkyns noted that "The law knows no favourites." When we speak of the rule of law, as early as the first century AD the Roman jurist Pliny the Younger was writing that "the Prince is not over the law, but the law is over the Prince." Yet the UK government is attempting to put itself and its agencies above the law whenever it suits them, robbing us not only of our claim to be a democratic and legal society but also of our hold on fundamental principles going back over the centuries.

The Rule of Law

One of the principal values underpinning British politics is the concept known as the rule of law. In 1885, the celebrated British jurist Albert Dicey published his *Introduction to the Study of the Law of the Constitution*, which came to be regarded as the authoritative text on British constitutional theory. In this text, Dicey described what he termed the three guiding principles of British constitutionalism: the sovereignty of Parliament, the conventions of the constitution, and the rule of law. Dicey argued that the rule of law was composed of three fundamental concepts:

> No one may be punished for any offence, nor suffer any form of penalty for a breach of the law unless it is proven in open court. That means that there can be no arbitrary power exercised by any official persons or bodies over individual citizens.
>
> All persons are equal before the law, regardless of economic, social and political status. There are no class distinctions and no one is above the law

> The rule of law includes the benefits and freedoms conferred on individuals by judicial decisions when determining individual and collective rights from the ordinary law of the land.

There can be little doubt that the measures we have just discussed by both Labour and Conservative coalition governments breach at least two, if not all three of Dicey's fundamental concepts. Given the important political value placed on the rule of law in the United Kingdom, it constitutes the basis of political and constitutional morality. Thus, ethical judgement of political behaviour primarily depends on how that behaviour meets the moral criteria embedded within this concept, and modern British governments can consequently be judged both unethical and unlawful in their actions. The rule of law is the principle of limited government, and the principle of curbing the power of officialdom, indeed preventing the use of excessive power by anyone in a polity. Power must only be exercised in a limited and legal context, never arbitrarily. In addition, what Dicey was proposing was not exactly new. Throughout history philosophers have argued that civilised society must be morally founded on rule by law, as opposed to rule by people exercising power. The Roman philosopher Cicero argued, "We are all servants of the laws in order that we may be free."

The Athenian statesman Pericles argued in what

The Rule of Law

is known as his "funeral oration", as reported by Thucydides, that:

> Our polity does not copy the laws of neighbouring states; we are rather a pattern to others than imitators ourselves. It is called a democracy, because not the few but the many govern. If we look to the laws, they afford equal justice to all in their private differences; if to social standing, advancement in public life falls to reputation for capacity, class considerations not being allowed to interfere with merit; nor again does poverty bar the way, if a man is able to serve the state, he is not hindered by the obscurity of his condition.
>
> Where the law is subject to some other authority and has none of its own, the collapse of the state, in my view, is not far off; but if law is the master of the government and the government is its slave, then the situation is full of promise and men enjoy all the blessings that the gods shower on a state.

And in 'Politics', Aristotle argues:

> It is more proper that law should govern than any one of the citizens: upon the same principle, if it is advantageous to place the supreme power in some particular persons, they should be appointed to be only guardians, and the servants of the laws.

History is littered by statements such as these

arguing that civilised societies must be governed by people who are themselves governed by laws applied equally to each individual. Today we call this concept the rule of law. What is significant for modern British government is that we can no longer pretend that our governments operate by this concept or even attempt to honour it. British society is no longer protected by the rule of law and is in breach of all Dicey's three guiding principles. We must also recognise that the primary motivation for abandoning the moral and ethical structure required by the principles underpinning the rule of law is an obsession with neo-liberal free market ideology. As legal and political systems reflect and are shaped by the economic system, and must operate in a manner that supports and protects the economic system, the corruption of legal and political systems results from a corrupt economic system. The rule of law, being a constraint on government and its agencies, threatens to limit the operations of neo-liberal interests. Neo-liberals argue that there must be a complete separation between government and economics, but in practice they want the former to be subservient to the latter. It is no accident that widespread corruption of the political system, the financial system, the press and the police etc. has happened under the influence of neo-liberal economic dominance. Corruption is always present in public life, but in modern Britain it has reached such scandalous levels that it has provoked widespread disgust and rioting.

It is the driving force behind increasing support for Scottish independence, and, as Martin Luther King so eloquently expressed it, rioting is the language of the unheard. Britain's politicians take little notice of public opinion unless it chimes with their own goals and they increasingly tolerate neither criticism nor challenge.

Dicey's description of the rule of law was the standard explanation until 2006, when the then senior law officer in Britain, Lord Thomas Bingham, gave the sixth Sir David Williams Lecture on the subject of "The Rule of Law". Bingham was concerned that the concept of the rule of law had become too vague and abstract since Dicey's day and that there was neither clear definition of it, nor agreement as to what it meant. He was also of the opinion that it is a dynamic and evolutionary concept that is subject to change and development. According to Bingham the rule of law means "that all persons and authorities within the state, whether public or private, should be bound by and entitled to the benefit of laws publicly made, taking effect (generally) in the future and publicly administered in the courts". He developed his version of the rule of law from principles expounded by John Locke in 1690 and Thomas Paine in 1776 when Locke stated that "Where-ever law ends, tyranny begins" and Paine stated that "in America THE LAW IS KING. For as in absolute governments the King is law, so in free countries the law ought to be King; and there ought to be no other."

Bingham expanded his analysis of the rule of law to include eight fundamental principles that determine if a state truly adheres to the rule of law or not. We do not need to highlight all eight principles but the most fundamental ones do concern us here – that "the law must be accessible and so far as possible intelligible, clear and predictable," and "questions of legal right and liability should ordinarily be resolved by application of the law and not the exercise of discretion." This is a restatement of the principle that law must not be exercised in an arbitrary fashion. He also insisted that "the laws of the land should apply equally to all, save to the extent that objective differences justify differentiation." As a result, equality before the law is rightly seen as a cornerstone of the constitution, and underpins the governmental and legal systems' claim to ethical and moral authority. For example, in 2001 the Labour government passed legislation under which the only terrorist suspects who could be detained indefinitely were foreigners. In response to this, Lord Scarman ruled that

> Habeas corpus protection is often expressed as limited to "British subjects". Is it really limited to British nationals? Suffice it to say that the case law has given an emphatic "no" to the question. Every person within the jurisdiction enjoys the equal protection of our laws. There is no distinction between British nationals and others. He who is subject to English law is entitled to its protection.

Lord Bingham registers his agreement with Scarman's ruling. Bingham then stresses that "ministers and public officers at all levels must exercise the powers conferred on them in good faith, fairly, for the purpose for which the powers were conferred, without exceeding the limits of such powers and not unreasonably," and "the law must afford adequate protection of fundamental human rights."

Bingham was a critic of those who oppose the European Convention on Human Rights and asked which of the convention rights they would discard, going on to ask, "Would you rather live in a country in which these rights were not protected by law?" Significantly, Bingham's eighth principle states that "the rule of law requires compliance by the state with its obligations in international law as in national law." On the basis of that eighth principle Bingham declared that Britain's invasion of Iraq in 2003 was unlawful. Restating his view that the rule of law constrains governments as well as individuals, Bingham concluded that "it seems to me that the rule of law does depend on an unspoken but fundamental bargain between the individual and the state, the governed and the governor, by which both sacrifice a measure of the freedom and power which they would otherwise enjoy." In January 2012, in the *Independent*, the President of the European Court of Human Rights, Sir Nicolas Bratza, criticised "senior British politicians" for their ignorance of the Court's history and legal position. He accused such politicians of pandering to the tabloid press and stated that the claims made in the UK by press and politicians against the Court are not borne out by the facts. Criticism of the Court of Human Rights by British politicians is another example of an arrogant British elite taking issue with anyone who dares to constrain their activities or challenge them in any way, and how they are not prepared to "sacrifice a measure of the freedom and power they would otherwise enjoy", which is in breach of the condition required by Lord Bingham for a nation complying with the rule of law.

Now that the government's behaviour is undermining its own authority, the concept of the rule of law is crucial, particularly for a nation like the United Kingdom that proudly claims to have upheld this rule for so long. Government derives its duties, responsibilities and all its authority from the people of the nation it governs. As a result, it must always be accountable, and removable. It does not have rights, only people have rights. Governments have authority which should be subject to the people. In addition, governments can not only lose their authority, but they can forfeit it by their own actions, particularly when they offend or deliberately ignore the rule of law. I hope to demonstrate that modern British governments breach all of the principles embodied in the rule of law. For example, in March 2010, the human rights organisation Amnesty International published a very damning report on Britain's attitude

The Rule of Law

to human rights, arguing that there is "credible evidence" of Britain's involvement in torture, unlawful detentions and rendition. Amnesty accuses the British government of a catalogue of "grave human rights violations" using the excuse of its "war on terror". At the time of writing, Britain has been guilty of imprisoning a Muslim man, Babar Ahmad, for seven years without trial. Throughout that seven years, Mr Ahmad has never been questioned by anybody about his alleged offences and has never had any evidence shown against him. This would be unacceptable behaviour for any nation, but in a nation that prides itself on legal process and adherence to the rule of law, charges of abuse of office and crimes against humanity should be brought against all the personnel responsible for this action, including the Prime Minister. This is the behaviour that the UK once associated with the Gestapo and the KGB. Other charges levelled in the Amnesty report are that Britain is guilty of concealing victims' complaints and failing to disclose evidence of torture. When confronted with such accusations, successive governments simply refuse to comment or give any answers other than issuing blanket denials. This report came twenty-four hours after Members of Parliament, in alliance with Amnesty International, Liberty and the American-based Human Rights Group, published a joint letter in the British press demanding an independent inquiry into Britain's role in relation to torture and rendition. What is significant about many of these allegations is that, if they are true, then government ministers must have signed warrants approving what are blatant unlawful acts by intelligence officers. In 1994 the UK Parliament passed the Intelligence Services Act which, under Section 7, protects British personnel who have committed criminal acts such as bugging phones, bribery, murder, kidnap or torture, as long as their actions have been authorised in writing by a government minister. Elected politicians have no right to refuse to answer legitimate questions concerning the legality of their actions, particularly those carried out in the name of the British people and which may have serious international consequences for the nation. It should never be forgotten that there were no threats of terror from Islamic groups until the British government launched terror on Islamic groups, communities and nations.

The above principles of law are all self-explanatory and concern the actions of both the American and British authorities. The American NDAA has been signed into law and has therefore been formalised. This Act breaches every one of the above principles and therefore denies the United States the right to claim to be a society governed by the rule of law. Those who glorify the USA and wish to ape its behaviour should stop and reflect on how a society that claims to be democratic can so speedily abandon some of its most cherished freedoms and liberties on the flimsiest of excuses. Both the American and British governments are telling their populations that they will be empowered to take action without being accountable for it, and will wage war against their own citizenry if they feel justified. These are two nations that fought in the greatest war in history against regimes that were doing precisely what they intend to do now. Following Britain's adoption of the free market economic model that has its genesis in the Chicago school economic policies championed by Milton Friedman and his supporters, Britain's economic system has increasingly looked to the United States for its inspiration. This has resulted in the British increasingly imitating American-style legal, social and political structures in order to successfully implement an economic model that is viewed as being the best for free market success. But most importantly Britain has adopted and promoted philosophical justifications for the behaviour associated with free market economic activity; philosophical concepts that are hostile to collectivist and state activity and very critical of what we will describe as positive rights and freedoms. It is this economic model and the policies it produces that are the driving force behind the measures we have just been discussing. Thus Britain is increasingly in breach of all the principles underpinning a law-abiding nation discussed by both Dicey and Lord Bingham. Both the British and American governments are justifying such draconian measures as necessary to the so-called "war on terror". Such measures are effectively acts of state terror. How can anyone fail to see arrest and incarceration without charge, without trial, without access to family or legal representation and without knowledge of possible release, as anything other than terror? Such measures are the essence of tyranny.

From a legal, constitutional, political and human dimension, this is a step too far. No government or individual has the right or authority to take such measures for any reason. This is a people, a society, freely giving up their claim to be truly human. Any rational person should be capable of appreciating the horror of this happening to any other human being – of being locked up without charge, without access to legal representation and with no discernible end in sight. Anyone who contemplates such a thing happening to them must appreciate that it could lead to the loss of their sanity. To be locked away with no knowledge of why you are being incarcerated, being interrogated and possibly tortured in the knowledge that there is no discernible end is a nightmare no one should be subjected to. At the time I am writing in April 2012, a British citizen, Shaker Aamer, has been incarcerated in Guantanamo Bay for over 10 years without charge and without trial. This is unlawful and a serious breach of human rights. It is in itself a form of torture. By endorsing measures such as these, and implementing NDAA, President Obama is forfeiting America's right to be called a civilised state, and the legislators who endorsed them, along with the people who carry out the measures described as taking place in Guantanamo Bay, and who are about to carry out further actions allowed under NDAA, are abandoning their place within civilised society. Our humanity is measured by our ability to empathise with and defend other people's rights, even when they hold very different views, defend different vested interests or even undermine these fundamental and inalienable rights under discussion here. In addition, the USA now systematically tortures people, including those who have never been charged or convicted of any crime. It is simply enough for the USA to suspect people of having possibly been involved, or thinking about being involved, in what they term a terrorist act. This contravenes the numerous treaties they have signed denouncing torture and pledging to uphold universal human rights, and even the American Constitution itself (the Eighth Amendment forbidding cruel and unusual punishment). For people in the UK, there is abundant evidence that we are complicit in torture and rendition, and that this has been endorsed at the highest levels of British government.

Human beings have the capacity to divest themselves of that essence we recognise as our humanity. According to Alexander Solzhenitsyn, humans can voluntarily take the irreversible step into what he calls "the bottomless pit" and therefore cease to be truly human beings. If you condemn another human being to exist without any consideration of their humanity, their dignity, their fears, their welfare, indeed their very life, you cannot yourself claim to possess the human spirit. If you torture another human being, inflict terror and indescribable pain, and take all hope and humanity from that person, totally dehumanising them, and do that with calculation and deliberation, then not only are you no longer entitled to be described as human, you are lower than any beast known to man. What constitutes the essence of the human being is their capacity for reason, for sympathy, for empathy, for recognising and respecting the essence of other human beings. It is summed up in the ethos of "love thy neighbour". Of course people can act irrationally and can violate other people's dignity and human rights. But the human being feels regret and shame, and tries to avoid doing it again. What we are examining here is organised and premeditated inhumanity, legalised official inhumanity. By offending against human decency, its own national law and constitution, and then compounding the felony by offending against international law and treaty, the United States is putting itself beyond the definition of civilised society, and this disease is affecting the British. It was reported in the *Guardian* on Sunday 8 April 2012 that a Libyan woman, Fatima Bouchar, and her husband, were detained in Bangkok in 2004, and flown to Libya by the Americans. Ms Bouchar was four and a half months pregnant at the time. The arrests of Ms Bouchar and her husband were instigated by the British, who were implicated in the couple's subsequent treatment by the American authorities. Now, the fundamental cornerstone of law and a civilised society is that a person is innocent until proven guilty. Once arrested by the British and Americans, Ms Bouchar was placed in a cell in Bangkok where her left wrist was chained to a wall and both her feet were chained to the floor. She was kept like that for four days, given water but no food, despite the fact that the Americans knew she was pregnant. After four days, three Americans, two men and a woman, who were dressed in black and wore black balaclavas, forced Ms Bouchar to lie on a stretcher where they bound her from head to toe in tape and took her onto a plane. She was taped to the stretcher for 17 hours unable to move. The tape was wound around her head and eyes, and then a hood and earmuffs were placed on her rendering her unable to move, hear or see. This was a person who had not been charged with anything, had not been questioned, had not been tried and had no explanation as to why this was happening. Can you imagine the horror and terror of being arrested like that and chained to a wall for four days, being completely immobilised, deprived of sound or vision for at least seventeen hours, and then being taken somewhere in a plane with no idea of where you're going and why? Bound head to foot, you're unable to move, urinate or defecate, unless you soil yourself. You have no water, food or indeed hope. This woman was pregnant and was given no food for four days and no sustenance of any kind for at least seventeen hours after that. Her terrors would have been compounded by her fears for her unborn child. American and British officials are supposed to consider people innocent until proven guilty, and it transpired that she was indeed innocent. Now this was all done with no explanation and before any form of interrogation took place. If that's not a definition of torture, then what on earth is? What does this say about our so-called civilised society and our security services, and what does it say about our politicians who sanction such treatment to people and then go home at night to their families, a nice meal, a gin and tonic and a good night's sleep? Are such British and American politicians and officials in essence any different from the Nazis or the KGB? This is terror, and any state that does such things is a terrorist state. It sends out a very clear signal that our authorities and their official agents have no concern or respect whatsoever for anyone's human rights.

We must never lose sight of what government is, what its functions and roles are, and, most importantly, what its limits are. Governments are made up of people like you and me who have decided to enter politics and are fortunate enough to have been elected to office; they have no special rights. Someone could be a teacher, or a cleaner, or a lawyer, or in any other form of work, indeed they could be unemployed, and the next day could find themselves a member of parliament. An unemployed person or cleaner could then prove to be every bit as effective as a member of parliament as a lawyer or teacher. There is no knowledge or skill required to be in government, no one requires any training; they only need to be able to harness a sufficient number of votes. But we are accustomed to assuming that governments do have rights; rights to do as they please; rights to take actions with no reference to the people who elect them. We have been hoodwinked into believing that politics is some kind of specialist skill and that politicians possess knowledge and abilities that prepare and equip them for their positions. Nothing could be farther from the truth. The only specialist skill that British politicians exhibit is the capacity to *lie* persistently through their teeth without the slightest twinge of conscience or regret. I repeat, governments have no rights; people have rights. This is important because if governments are allowed to, they will eventually decide to deny the people one of their most fundamental rights – the right to elect politicians into and out of office – and therefore to dispense with the bothersome process of election. Governments are public employees. The public hire them, pay their wages, support and sustain them; that is why governments are derivative. A government has a material foundation; it exists because it fulfills a function, to represent the wishes and needs of the people who elect it. The word government comes from the Latin word *gubernare*, to govern. The Latin in its turn takes the word *gubernare* from the Greek *kubernetes*. In Greek a *kubernetes* was the pilot of a ship, the steersman or the helmsman. So government is the art of steering, of guiding and governing the ship of state. These Greek and Latin roots were translated into the English as governor, or ruler. Thus, elections for the post of a governor, particularly in the United States, are known as gubernatorial elections. Government arises out of the social, interactive and interdependent nature of the human being, and being in government does not give you the right to do exactly as you please, unaccountable to the people who put you in government in the first place. In modern Britain, government has abandoned its role of representing the nation and the people in favour of class and elite interests. Genuine recovery for the British economy and civil society must be preceded by a radical reform of the British political system. British government is wholly unrepresentative, and staffed by a self-serving and self-perpetuating elite that constitutes a form of heredity. The traditional constraints on British government no longer operate effectively and the British need a proper constitution that codifies and formalises their rights as citizens. British government is heavily dependent on trust to maintain its authority and its legitimacy, and that trust is evaporating due to the incompetence, greed and outright criminality of successive governments. Since 1979, successive British governments have ruled by blatant class warfare, which led to serious rioting in British cities in the summer of 2011. These riots are a sign of what is to come unless political and economic priorities are altered, and I have no confidence that such changes will occur. To dismiss such events as the 2011 riots as sheer criminality, as all official accounts have done, is to deny reality.

Lord Acton famously noted that "power tends to corrupt, and absolute power corrupts absolutely." In the UK we have a political system where people get voted into office under the auspices of the party system, and for many of them it becomes a job for life. They become corrupted by the power that comes with office, particularly when that office is largely unaccountable. A British politician has to go through the tedious process of regular election, but it is not they who are being elected; it is their party, for whom they are little more than a cypher. Too many British politicians are of the opinion that the office they are elected to is theirs! They have a right to it; it belongs to them. In government there is a belief that those elected are somehow special and superior to the common man, that they have a right not only to guide the ship of state, but to control its every movement. This is compounded by the class system, whereby a political elite recruit their successors from that same elite. From an early age they progress through an elite education system that socialises them into believing that they are indeed different and entitled to govern. They then progress into leading universities which groom them for elite recruitment into a privileged form of employment that will prepare them for election to the highest offices of state. Simples!! If there is one thing certain about our representative democracy in the UK, it is that British politicians represent no one but themselves and their class. Our representative democracy is a farce and a disgrace – a self-perpetuating elite minority of public schoolboys. This elite group of so-called experts are so expert, competent and effective that they have endangered the political structure of the United Kingdom by causing the Scots and Welsh and increasingly the Cornish people to demand more and more self-determination and responsibility. They have collapsed the financial system and caused a crisis in our relations with the European Union, the Middle East, Iraq, Iran and Afghanistan. If that were all, it would be bad enough, but they are increasingly a danger to their own population. This expert elite has demonised the working class, single parents, the unemployed, people on benefits, the disabled, significant ethnic groups, black people and Muslims. It passes ever more repressive measures to protect itself from challenge and from the repercussions of its own greed, corruption and incompetence. These actions stem from an arrogant belief that the Anglo-American way of life – its culture, and its political, social and economic systems as interpreted by its elite class – are so self-evidently superior to all other models that it has a duty to impose them, not only on its own people but also on the rest of the world, if the rest of the world is too stupid to recognise them and embrace them. That is why its members exhibit open hatred and contempt for their own people if they happen to be working class, or adhere to a different culture than that espoused by the elite. The ruling classes in both the United Kingdom and the United States will not be challenged, and, if any challenge is mounted by people who believe they are exercising their fundamental human rights, then those human rights will have to be constrained and/or removed.

Human Rights

Human rights are rights we have achieved by the fact of being human. They may be formalised by other humans in legal documents or constitutions, but they are not grants, or the gifts of enlightened rulers, nor are they bestowed by a deity and enshrined in religious writings. They stem from the obvious empirical fact that all human beings are born equal. All humans enter the world the same way and by the same method; there are no social distinctions, no rank nor privilege in the birth process. Once in the world, all human beings are in the same state of helplessness and totally dependent on other human beings for their survival. Without that support no human would last more than a few hours. That is an obvious and incontestable fact; it is almost the only fact that I would venture to call a truth. Humans are social beings; that is their nature. From the moment of their birth they are dependent on other humans and, as they grow and develop, they continue to be dependent on, learn from and interact with other humans. As a result, such interaction necessarily brings cooperation with each other, which comes naturally. Twenty people will overcome a mammoth in a hunt for food far more effectively than one or two. Because of their social nature humans divide their labour, they don't all rush in and charge at the mammoth getting in each other's way, they learn from other animals how to gang up on, and overcome, much larger prey. This means that they divide their labour, and the daily tasks of living and providing food and shelter, between each other. This process of dividing tasks and specialising in different factors of production raises everyone's standard of living. This then brings an understanding of reciprocal need and the need for mutual respect and protection. Human evolution was accompanied by an evolution of insight (we call it common sense) into what we gain from mutual respect and cooperation and the dangers of conflict and destructive self-interest. Now, human beings are in conflict with each other all the time; if we disagree with each other about anything we are, by definition, in conflict with each other. However, not all conflict and self-interest is destructive, that is obvious; indeed human conflict in everyday life is a major factor driving meaningful social change, because humans regulate conflict, institutionalise it and devise regulatory methods for solving it, making conflict both positive and progressive when dealt with in that very human manner. But what is also obvious is that the self-interest encouraged by free market economic theory and its political bedfellow, right-wing libertarian ideology, most certainly is destructive and divisive. It is destructive of society and of its necessary structures, particularly when the governing elite engages in deregulating every obstacle to its success and attacks the structures designed to control destructive human activity.

Human beings are reflective creatures. They can reflect on their actions, thoughts, beliefs and experience. They can therefore learn and adapt; they can change and progress. If their hunt for the mammoth goes badly and they lose their lunch, or if the mammoth turns on them and inflicts injuries, they can reflect and adapt their hunting technique to ensure success on the next hunt. They learn from experience, a process we call empiricism. The knowledge and learning they gain from their experience is empirical knowledge, the safest and surest way for humans to progress. Our mutual support of each other opens the way to the most basic right of all, the right to life. That right should be granted to us at birth by the human instinct to care for and nurture a newborn. As we are brought into the world and survive by the efforts of others, we then reciprocate and perform such services to other people to ensure the survival of our children and future generations. We have a right to life, because if that right was not honoured when we were born, then we would be the last generation of humanity and the human species would perish. We therefore have a duty as a human being to respect the right of everyone else to their life as well. As we enter into the world completely helpless and require constant care for our survival, we have a right to be nourished, clothed and sheltered. We have such rights because we continually grant them to each individual born; they are communal rights, species rights, human rights, and, as experience teaches us, necessary for the survival of the species. As a result, such equal rights belong to everyone who has ever lived or ever will live. With rights come responsibilities, and our greatest responsibility is to recognise and respect the rights of each other. We develop, through experience, the capacity to formulate and understand general principles that enable us to live and flourish in a communal manner because we understand the social nature of human existence. Each of us possesses such rights simply by our existence as a human being, and we have a duty to recognise and respect the rights of all others because they exist on the same equal basis that we do. From this beginning, other rights follow, such as the right to freedom and liberty, because without freedom and liberty the concept of rights becomes meaningless. Life must be meaningful, because if it is meaningless then it has no purpose. If we respect the right to life, but refuse the rights of freedom and liberty, refuse to give that life any meaning, then life will speedily descend into mere existence. A slave doesn't live; he or she simply exists – for the benefit of other people.

Some people call such rights natural rights, but

some thinkers have confused the debate on natural rights by identifying them with "God", "the gods" or other metaphysical concepts. This implies that we do not have such rights by our human existence but by the gift of some supernatural entity to whom we must be eternally grateful, and we may forfeit them if some human representatives of a god decide we have offended the god's principles. I will therefore simply refer to them as human rights or organic rights. As a result, no one, no group, no class, no elite, no government has the right to deny us our rights to life, freedom and liberty, and all have a duty to respect and honour them. Each of us has the human right to provide for ourselves, and to feed, clothe and shelter ourselves and our dependants. Should any human institution, such as a social class or a government, so order society as to prevent us exercising those rights, then they must make other provision. Political and civil rights are therefore a reflection and extension of our human rights, and, in the modern world, this has profound implications for welfare and the distribution of wealth.

Modern Britain is the result of a historical process that began with the Norman Conquest. Through this process we have reached an empirical reality whereby one per cent of the UK population own seventy per cent of the land. This development is also the reason for the class structure of the UK whereby much of that land is owned by the monarchy, the church and an aristocratic elite. If the system of ownership and control denies people access to land that can sustain them and provide for their food, and a legal system upholds the heredity basis of legalised theft, creating a modern economy entirely dependent on money where the vast majority rely on an employer for a money wage, and then significant sections of the population can't find work and don't have enough money to live on as determined by the norm for that society, which also progressively denies them a sufficient level of benefits that are the only other method whereby they can enjoy a basic standard of living, then significant numbers of people will acquire the money necessary to them by other means. That normally means that they will acquire it by methods that the dominant value system labels as criminal. Such people would be quite right to do so!

Why? Because, in a modern society like the UK, operating under a capitalist economic system that entrenches politically, legally, and socially, the rights of private property but refuses to admit that people have a right to employment, then the state must provide the unemployed with alternative funds to sustain a reasonable standard of living. The system of ownership has its genesis in military conquest and has been sustained by legalised theft and systematic fraud, which has evolved into so-called property rights. However, with rights come obligations, and, if your rights have been gained by denying your fellow human beings the fundamental means to sustain their life, then you are obliged to provide an alternative. As a result, if the capitalist class of property owners and employers cannot, or will not, provide sufficient means of employment and money wages to the population, then the state must do so, as it is this state that is upholding and supporting that economic system. Should both the employer class and the state fail to do so, then people have the right to take from that class and the state whatever they require to sustain their lives and their welfare, as long as by doing so they do not endanger anyone else's life, and, if the ruling class and the state seek to prevent them by force, then they are perfectly entitled to reciprocate. In such a circumstance, government and the state are exceeding their authority, which is the protection and welfare of the people, and, if they proceed to wage war against the populace on behalf of a minority interest that is refusing people their fundamental rights, then they no longer have any authority and the people have the right to overthrow them, along with the elite class directing such war against the mass of the population.

The free market economic system is based on the fundamental precept of the right to property. This is a highly debatable point as human beings argued for centuries that other human beings were their property and that they had a right to dispose of such property as they saw fit. This is of course the justification for slavery. So, such a statement is too general and ambiguous to be accepted as a precept in its own right. As we are all born equal and require the produce of the land to provide our food and therefore sustain our life, we all must have a fundamental right to property in the form of land. Try telling that to the British royal family, or the Anglican and Catholic churches! Given the structure of society in a modern world, this is obviously not a viable option, and it is not one that most people would desire anyway. However, this does not negate the fundamental point that we all have a right to life, its maintenance and sustenance, and also to provide for those, such as our children, who are dependent on us. What the free market theory of capitalism does, however, is turn the right to property into a right of ownership and control established by conquest and theft that supersedes everyone else's right. Modern law argues that if you own land, then you have the right to do what you wish with it and dispose of it as you see fit. This clearly conflicts with the definition of equality established in this essay. Another argument is that such people have a moral right to that property (that is one of my objections to the notion of natural law, as too many thinkers base their notion of natural law on metaphysical appeals to a god or gods) and that to challenge that is to challenge a form of divine law (it is God's Will). However, if we wish to appeal to divine law and authority, let us take the dominant Christian thinking as a guide to the notion of a natural right to property and see what the Bible says on such a subject, given that our ruling classes regularly appeal to religion as their authority and claim that the UK is a Christian country.

The Book of Leviticus contains the fundamental biblical laws governing ownership and control of land. Chapter 25 explains what is known as the Year of Jubilee. The Year of Jubilee began every fiftieth year on the Day of Atonement, as the Day of Atonement symbolises liberty and freedom. Leviticus 25:1-2 tells us:

> And the Lord spake unto Moses in mount Sinai, saying, / Speak unto the children of Israel, and say unto them, When you come into the land which I give you, then shall the land keep a Sabbath unto the Lord.

He then instructs them that they are allowed to work the land for the first six years, but the seventh year must be set aside as a Sabbath when they must leave the land free to rest for one year. Then in verse 8 He instructs them that they must count seven of these Sabbath years, which makes forty-nine years from when they arrived in the Promised Land. The following year, the fiftieth, is to be a special one, the Year of Jubilee. Leviticus 25:8-10 tells us:

> And thou shalt number seven Sabbaths of years unto thee, seven times seven years; and the space of the seven Sabbaths of years shall be unto thee forty and nine years / Then shalt thou cause the trumpet

of the jubilee to sound on the tenth day of the seventh month, in the day of atonement shall ye make the trumpet sound throughout all your land/ And ye shall hallow the fiftieth year and proclaim liberty throughout all the land unto all the inhabitants thereof: it shall be a jubilee unto you; and ye shall return every man unto his possession, and ye shall return every man unto his family

As a result, we find that divine law requires that "ye shall return every man unto his possession" and forbids the possession of land that was not originally yours by right on a permanent basis. All land sales are temporary; they are actually what we today call leases, because, even if you have legally purchased my land from me on an agreed and amicable basis, you must return it to me, or my family, free of charge at the jubilee. Therefore, under God's law, you are not allowed to sell your land on a permanent basis because it is your family's inheritance. If you sell your land it will revert to you, and if you buy land from someone who has fallen into debt or for whatever reason causes them to sell it, you lose it back to their family in the year of jubilee. Thus no one can permanently lose their land inheritance through debt. At the Jubilee, the land reverts back to them, and any remaining debts are cancelled. Leviticus 25: 23–28 tells us:

> The land shall not be sold forever; for the land is mine; for ye are strangers and sojourners with me /

> And in the land of your possession ye shall grant a redemption for the land / If thy brother be waxen poor, and hath sold away some of his possession, and if any of his kin come to redeem it, then shall he redeem that which his brother sold / And if the man have none to redeem it, and himself be able to redeem it; Then let him count the years of the sale thereof, and restore the overplus unto the man to whom he sold it; that he may return unto his possession. But if he be not able to restore it to him, then that which is sold shall remain in the hand of him that bought it until the year of jubilee; and in the jubilee it shall go out, and he shall return unto his possession.

Here we find a divine instruction that would put the fear of death into the landed property-owning classes and speculators who believe they have a right to do whatever they wish with their landed property, and have the right to pass it down through inheritance for as long as they are able, or to extract the maximum profit they are capable of extracting. It also blows a hole in the theory of the modern concept of a natural right to property! Under Mosaic law, everyone has a natural right to property, and, if you sell land, any of your family have the right to buy it back at any time. You yourself have the right to buy it back at any time. However, even if no one can afford to redeem their land, it automatically returns to their family free of charge at the Jubilee.

How do you like them apples, your majesty and all your aristocratic friends? How does that sound, our noble one per cent? In Biblical Israel, land value was based on the value of barley (Leviticus 27:16) with "an homer" of barley seed valued at "fifty shekels of silver". Thus, if you wished to buy land, it was priced at the amount of barley the land under purchase would be able to produce from the date of purchase to the year of Jubilee. As a result, if anyone wished to redeem the land that had previously been sold, the price was fixed by this mechanism for both buyer and seller. In other words, it was regulated and did not allow for speculation. There was no profit there I'm afraid, and indeed there was no market pricing, the value of land was fixed and not open to speculation. Regardless of how many years remained until the next jubilee, whether it was forty-eight, thirty, twenty or five, then the value of that land was decided by the same formula. Both buyer and seller knew the price they would have to pay, and that was fixed and beyond debate. In addition, for those people who believe they have the right to deny access to their land; under God's law the poor were legally allowed, not only to access the land, but to eat in the fields by gathering grain and fruit by hand. This would be condemned today as theft, and such an instruction as communist. What were you saying about a return to Christian values, Mr Prime Minister? What do so-called Christian priests, ministers and clerics who uphold the property rights of royalty and the propertied classes, and control millions of acres of land that are owned by their various churches think when they read things like this in the book they spend their entire lives trying to convince people is the sacred word of their god? I await a response!! Where does this notion of a right to property come from? It comes from those who exercise power, both physical and mental, and have the ability to establish such a right by force and propaganda. Such people control the decision-making processes and therefore control the legislative processes, they form a class and make law in the interests of that class. Such rights become absolute rights, not because God says so, but because the law says so.

Freedom and Rights

When discussing the concepts of freedom and liberty, we will simply refer to freedom, as for our purposes, both words signify the same thing. The concepts of freedom and rights are not unproblematic. For example, the neo-liberal agenda continually stresses that freedom is the ultimate human condition and must be the ultimate goal of both politics and economics. This leads them to emphasise that the continual goal of government policies must be to restore and maintain individual freedom, and in this context it is important to remember that to the neo-liberal this primarily means economic freedom. Here the waters become muddied as, taken literally, individual freedom is a meaningless concept. Individual freedom is indeed a basic human right, but has to be seen in the context of the human being as a social animal, in that, one person's exercise of freedom may require the restriction of another's, and, in economic terms, one person's use of scarce resources may mean another person's lack of resources. That is unavoidable and simply a fact of social life. To discuss the concepts of freedom and rights in an abstract, desocialised way can be a futile exercise, and it is meaningless in the context of the human being as an atomised individual. For example, the philosopher Thomas Hobbes states that:

> Liberty, or freedom, signifies, properly, the absence of opposition; by opposition, I mean external impediments of motion. A freeman is he; that in those things, which by his strength and wit he is able to do, is not hindered to do what he has a will to do.

That statement looks quite impressive, but what does it actually mean? Am I having my freedom impeded by being physically and/or legally prevented from killing someone if that is what I have a will to do? Clearly this is not what Hobbes intended by his statement, but it serves to highlight just how abstract and ambiguous such a statement is, and unfortunately how it is too often taken in that literal sense. If however Hobbes really does mean that freedom is an absence of opposition, he must mean that my freedom is being impeded when I am prevented from murdering someone against my will. The English philosopher Jeremy Bentham takes Hobbes's principle further by arguing that "liberty is the silence of the law." Therefore any law preventing me from murdering someone if that is my will must be restricting my liberty. Indeed Bentham states that "every law is an evil, because every law is a violation of liberty; so that government, I say again, can only choose between evils" (*Theories of Legislation*). He qualifies this by stating that, if, for example, government passes a law to prevent or punish me for murder, then they must ensure that the events that they seek to prevent are really evil, and such evils are greater than the evil they are about to employ as a means of prevention. According to Bentham's criteria, preventing a murder, or any other form of crime, is in itself an evil, but it may not be as evil as the actual murder or other crime. If that is the case, then preventing rape or preventing a terrorist blowing up a crowd of shoppers in a city centre *must be forms of evil*. This a peculiar interpretation of evil, and this philosophical thinking is therefore similar to the Objectivist philosophy of Ayn Rand who argues that altruism is evil – by altruism *she* means doing anything that may help or assist another if there is no benefit or advantage in it for you. It is this philosophy that is the guiding philosophical thought underpinning neo-liberalism. Another aspect of this way of defining freedom is the position taken by the philosopher Karl Popper, who argues that the state is a necessary evil and must not be allowed to grow greater than is absolutely necessary. What I will argue is that the state is neither good nor evil, but essentially reflects the policies and behaviour of the personnel in charge of it at any given point in history. The state is not a "thing" independent of human activity and behaviour; it is an interdependent set of human institutions, an administrative concept for the regulation and administration of any given political entity. People can be evil and can utilise the agencies of the state for evil purposes, but equally, people can be altruistic and concerned for the welfare of others and can therefore utilise the agencies of the state for good. The state can be large, small, intrusive or liberating; it can be whatever the people directing its activities desire it to be.

I was born into a very working class environment and for the first twelve years of my life lived in tenement accommodation rented from private landlords. The first six years were spent in accommodation with no electricity, and the first twelve were spent in accommodation with no inside toilet or hot water. I then discovered a new magical existence. We moved to a council house with inside toilet, a bath and hot water provided by a coal fire which heated a boiler in the house. When it was nice weather and we did not need a fire, we had an immersion heater to heat the water. We no longer needed to boil water in a kettle or a pan for washing purposes. Such luxuries were things I had only seen in films before. However, this house also had a garden - paradise! We could grow vegetables, not enough to sustain us all year, but I'm sure the reader will understand the cultural and psychological effects such changes have, not only on people, but on society at large. All this was only possible because of state intervention and the empowerment of local authorities to provide such facilities.

If I were asked to select one single measure in the history of the United Kingdom that could be presented as definitive in showing that the UK had finally matured as a civilised society, the answer would be the introduction of council housing. Council housing had enormous social and health benefits for the working people of this society. It gave people space, sanitary living conditions, the ability to express their own personality in the design and environment of their homes, and a real sense of dignity and belonging. Council housing eventually led to central heating, double glazing etc. even for the unemployed, and those unable to provide such things for themselves, the sick, the disabled and the elderly. Their rents and rates not only secured their accommodation, but also ensured repairs and maintenance, refuse collection, street lighting, and all the benefits of communal interests.

But perhaps the most important benefit was that it freed working people from the tyranny of the market in those areas of their lives. They were able to enjoy a quality of accommodation and services previously denied them. Years later, this was to arouse the hatred of free marketeers and opponents of positive rights towards council housing and council house tenants. War was declared on council housing and public services in general, and the state, under the domination of free-market thinkers determined to reinforce market disciplines on the whole of Britain as far as possible and at every opportunity. The Conservative Party was set on destroying the system of council-house provision by encouraging people to buy their council houses and forbidding any new council house building to replace those being privatised. Another motivation of the free-marketeers was to bring the council-house buyer once again under the tyranny of the market, and use the sale of council houses as a tool to divorce working people from their trades unions, as the majority of council house tenants were working people and most of them unionised. By purchasing their council house they would be subject to a mortgage and therefore most reluctant to take any form of industrial action, such as going on strike, for any reason that would cause them to fall into deficit, or even default, on their mortgage payments. This produced hostility to trades unions amongst newly empowered house-owners and caused mass defections from union membership in case such people were called out on strike. It worked.

However, not only did state-provided housing raise my standard of living, I then benefited from state-sponsored benefits to help me better myself. I got fed up working as an engineering machinist and decided to get some of the qualifications I never achieved at school. I was the son of a single parent and staying on at school to get higher qualifications that may help me to go to university had not been an option, as my mother needed me to work and earn a living. No complaints, as she sacrificed her whole life for me. However, thanks to new thinking about the roles and functions of the state, for the first time in British history further and higher education became available for someone from my background, even though at that point I took the decision not to access it. Some fifteen years later, as a married man with two children, I was able to go to night classes at my local further education college and study for higher qualifications courtesy of my local authority. Successfully gaining the required qualifications, I took the difficult decision, with the agreement of my family, that I should quit work as an engineering machinist and go to university. I was able to do this because I had access to a maintenance grant and travelling expenses. It was financially very difficult, but possible. It would have been impossible for me without the grant. Following my degree I was then able, again with state help, to gain a Master's degree.

I am eternally grateful to the state system that helped me in this way. But I am not unique; a whole generation was helped. Every member of the British government and all members of parliament had access to exactly the same benefits I enjoyed when I had access to them; and most of them accessed it regardless of family circumstances. The Labour Prime Minister Tony Blair admitted on public television that he went through university on the full maintenance grant, the same grant he was determined that no one else would have access to. His Chancellor

Gordon Brown accessed university exactly the same way Blair and I did. Those state-sponsored social provisions available to Blair and Brown enabled them to gain a higher education that allowed them to study the free-market doctrines they would then employ to damn such state-sponsored provisions and remove them from the public. They used them to reach the highest offices of state and make themselves very rich in the process. This was right and good for Blair and Brown, but far too good for anyone else unless they were already able to afford it. This is class politics, and an object lesson on the selfishness and hypocrisy of the elite.

After council housing, the free-marketeers were determined to subject another area of social life, this time education, to the disciplines of the market. An interesting insight into the free-market obsessed class nature of British society was provided by a gentleman called Mark Littlewood who, in September 2010, was a prominent free-market economist at the Institute of Economic Affairs, which describes itself as a "free-market think tank". It was reported in the *Independent* on 15 September 2010 that Mr Littlewood argued that the new coalition government of Tories and Liberal Democrats elected in May of 2010, should stop the public funding of libraries because he didn't use them. I don't use them, so why should I pay for them? – he asked. Surprise, surprise, one month later it was estimated that over a thousand libraries might have to be closed by local authorities because of the government's spending cuts. This is barbarism. This is the selfishness that our current political culture considers inevitable. I have been very fortunate with my health and had very little cause to use the National Health Service. I have paid the full insurance contributions all my adult working life, and do not mind one bit. I will gladly pay my share in the hope that I never need to access it. However, perhaps I should be like Mark Littlewood and call for the public funding of hospitals to end because I never use them. Make no mistake: that is what is coming to Britain if this dominant ideology is not challenged. I am not disabled and I don't have cancer or Parkinson's Disease, so why should my money go to help treat all those people who do?

That such questions are even asked and have to be challenged in modern Britain shows the extent of the true disease of British society, the spread of greed and selfishness. A dominant ideology of aggressive individual selfishness will produce aggressively selfish individuals. As a result, another area of public provision, health provision, came under the scrutiny of free-marketeers and they determined that health should also be subject to market discipline. If there is any area of public life that displays the benefits of intervention by the state and regulation, it is in health and welfare. If empirical data displays anything, it shows that the major contributions to public health and welfare came, not from the medical profession but from politics, in the form of legislation.

The requirements of legislation for the provision of sewage systems, drainage, clean water systems, public toilets, inside toilets, council housing with internal plumbing and baths, the requirement for toilets fitted with 's' bends and other such regulations have done as much and more to remove the causes of disease and illness as any medical measures. Industrial legislation in the form of health and safety legislation, controlling pollution, asbestos, requiring air extraction, limiting exposure to dangerous chemicals and a host of other measures have also contributed to the health and welfare of the population. Legislation limiting hours of work, the provision of school meals and milk, providing factories and schools with canteens, massively benefited the health and welfare of working people and their children. I could go on and on, but hope that this is sufficient to show that such forms of preventative and protective regulations are incalculable in their effectiveness as a provision for public health and welfare. History records such measures, but with little comment on their effects, or little research into their success in combatting disease and raising living standards.

Every one of the measures just discussed have been attacked by the free-marketeers, and if they haven't been removed or transferred to the private sector they soon will be. Indeed Margaret Thatcher first came to prominence in politics when she removed the provision of free milk from schoolchildren.

Freedom and Rights

In 2004 in England, the number of homeless households topped 200,000. By 2009 this had fallen to 60,000, which is to be welcomed, but it is no cause for celebration that 60,000 households are still homeless. Now, working on the basis that each household contains an average of 2.4 people, this means that 144,000 men, women and children in England alone were homeless in 2009. This situation is shown to be quite scandalous when we find out that in mid-2008, the Empty Homes Agency disclosed that there were 667,000 properties lying empty in England. Free market ideology is premised on concepts such as Thatcher's notion that there is no such thing as society and Littlewood's argument that you should not have to pay for anyone else to use a service. This then raises the question of what happens to people who cannot look after themselves in the market place, such as the unemployed, the sick and the disabled. Free-market health depends on private health insurance. The American experience that the free marketeers constantly hold up as their shining example, shows us how at any given time, there is an average of forty seven million Americans who do not have health insurance (that was the figure given by President Obama). In the United States, the healthcare industry is indifferent to the human costs of its actions in a relentless drive for profit. There are many people the private sector just refuses to insure as they are too expensive, whilst others are too poor to afford it. I recommend everyone to watch Michael

Moore's exposé of the American health system, *Sicko*. In June 2009, Wendell Potter, a former senior executive at the giant US healthcare firm Cigna, testified to a Senate Committee that the business practices of US healthcare firms push up costs, refuse to pay out as often as they can when patients get sick, and buy politicians. Potter told the Committee, "I worked as a senior executive at health insurance companies and I saw how they confuse their customers and dump the sick: all so they can satisfy their Wall Street investors." Commenting on Michael Moore's *Sicko*, Potter stated that it "hit the nail on the head". "The Michael Moore movie that I saw was full of truth." However, the free-marketeers are wrong, society is a reality and the state has a very important part to play in that society, as long as it remains accountable to the people and is properly regulated.

I argue that the people charged by the electorate with the control and direction of the state in modern Britain have lost their control and have allowed the personnel charged with its administration to become its directors, pursuing policies and programmes that should be the remit of the elected representatives of the polity. The state has become deregulated. In addition, you can only interpret the state as *necessarily* a force for evil if you elevate this particular concept of freedom to a moral absolute, that is, believe all restrictions on wilful human actions are by definition evil, but some are permissible as they may be less evil than the actions they are designed to restrict, and if you also interpret all state actions as limitations on your freedom, never as mechanisms to enhance your freedom. You can only reach such conclusions if you also believe that every restriction on your ability to act is a restriction on your freedom, and that such restrictions are always, by definition immoral, that is, they are always wrong, but sometimes less wrong than the behaviour they are designed to prevent. Thus, to maintain a consistent philosophical argument you must then go on to argue that complete human freedom requires a situation where there is neither government nor the state, nor any form of legislation whatsoever, as no state, governmental action or legislation can ever be interpreted as good and beneficial, only as the lesser evil. And finally, you can only advocate such views if you begin with the philosophical assumption that humans are rational beings who always act, not only in their own interests, but in their own best interests – in other words that they always know what is in their best interests. You must also reject the concept that people are normally dominated by their emotional impulses, by their affective interests. This line of thought of course reduces to absurdity but it is the logical conclusion of the advocacy of what we call *negative* freedom separated from the concept of the human being as a social animal. However, what is interesting is that none of the thinkers who advocate such views will admit to advocating the absence of the state. In the final analysis they grant a grudging role for the state and the organisation of politics. When you do apply rational thinking, then you are forced to admit that such a scenario is an impossibility, because you have to accept that the human being is a social (and therefore a regulatory) being.

Thus humans are socialised into internalising social norms and values. These norms and values we call a nation's culture, and that culture is an organic form of regulation, it grows out of the reality of social life in any social situation. In the United Kingdom it is a social norm to drive on the left side of the road. That is a restriction on your freedom to drive on the right side of the road, if it is your will to do so. Who decided that the British should drive on the left-hand side of the road? I have no idea, and it is irrelevant to me, because it works. It may restrict my freedom to drive on the right-hand side of the road if I have a will to do so, but it also ensures my safety. So how on earth can that be considered an evil? Indeed, respecting such social norms becomes a type of moral imperative, as each of us is dependent on everyone else respecting such norms for our own health and safety. Thus, rather than regarding such a restriction as a constraint on our freedom of action, it should be regarded as bestowing freedom. Restricting our freedom to drive however we wish to drive gives everyone else freedom of mind and life. Restricting the freedom to own and control slaves gives real human beings real and actual freedom. How can that be considered evil? When you consider the notion that the state is a necessary evil, and that all legislation is a form of evil, you can only conclude that this approach to freedom is actually nonsensical and a negation of what I have termed the derivative nature of government. It is also a denial of the social nature of the human species. The interdependent and interactive nature of human life means that some forms of human behaviour and action must be restricted and subject to constraints and regulation. That is the nature of the human being and human life, and such reality cannot be interpreted as evil. As I have already noted, it can become evil (and I find much of the legislation that governs my life to be distasteful, and deeply object to some of it) but it is not essentially so. Thus, a real and empirical state of human freedom requires some forms of human activity and behaviour to be restricted, such as the buying and selling of other human beings, and driving any way we want to on the roads. We may argue for freedom in the market, but we must never allow for a free market in human beings, so again the unqualified notion of a free market is nonsensical. Markets can never be properly free, nor should they be; all human interactive behaviour must be subject to regulation where necessary and appropriate. The concept of freedom from constraint cannot be regarded as an absolute. It is significant that Popper has to admit that the state is necessary, and this is a consistent problem for all advocates of this view, because, if there is a recognition that the state is necessary, then there is also an implicit recognition that complete freedom is impossible, because the state is a regulatory mechanism and confirmation that in real society human beings regulate themselves and their environment. As a result, complete freedom is not only impossible; it is not even desirable. One of the greatest of evils, according to the advocates of freedom as a moral absolute, is taxation, which they argue is a coercive limitation on your freedom to dispose of your wealth as you will. However, if you admit to the necessity of the state, then you must submit to the necessity for taxation, as the regulatory and administrative state agencies could not exist without it. Thus Popper can only conclude that the state is necessary, but his socialisation and class position (his milieu) cannot allow him to admit that the state can also be a source of good in the right hands, and therefore impels him to the conclusion that it is a necessary evil. I find this argument and this concept of freedom to be both contradictory and unacceptable. If the state is evil, it is a reflection of the people in control of it, but it is neither necessarily nor essentially so.

The debate on freedom (and indeed rights) concerns the differences between negative and positive freedom. Very crudely, the main difference is that negative freedom stresses freedom *from*, whilst positive freedom stresses freedom *to*. Both statements by Hobbes and Bentham are examples of the concept of "negative" freedom. At its most basic, the concept of negative freedom can be summarised as "non-interference". It signifies the absence of obstacles or constraints on human action and behaviour. In addition, negative freedom is almost always associated with individual action and behaviour. That is why I have emphasised the social nature of the human being, for negative freedom is normally associated with ideas and concepts that are hostile to collectivism and our social nature. Thus, taken to its logical conclusion, a policy-driven agenda fixated solely on considerations of negative freedom is essentially anti-social. It can lead to embracing philosophically dangerous concepts like Objectivism and economically dangerous concepts such as neoliberalism. Combine the two and you have a recipe for disaster. That is what we witnessed with the financial crisis that hit the Western world in 2008. By allowing business and finance to operate with as few restrictions and obstacles to their liberty as possible, by deregulating constraints on their behaviour as far as possible, these sectors were allowed to inflict immense harm and damage on the majority of the population, and to the institutions of the state. At the same time, we witnessed the damage inflicted on the social life and culture of the nation by the removal of constraints on the behaviour of the press when sections of the press, particularly the tabloid press, embarked on the large-scale illegal activity that was exposed by the phone hacking scandal, and which damaged many individuals as well as the social fabric of the nation. Consistent with this approach, all employment rights are seen as restrictions on the freedom of entrepreneurs and business, and so the state, under the direction of the neo-liberals and their persistent demands for freedom, has systematically diluted and removed the rights of working people. The business and financial sectors have been given the freedom to act as they see fit, whilst employees have seen their freedoms seriously restricted and their life chances seriously eroded. Under the guise of freedom, the business sector demands unrestricted freedom of action, including the freedom to beggar their workforce, destroy their terms and conditions of employment, and inflict large-scale unemployment and poverty, whilst the working people are denied the same independence if they seek to take action to protect their freedoms. As we said earlier, one person's freedom may require the limitation of another's. All actions by working people that seek to limit the power of the employer are branded as unacceptable; business freedom of action is considered to be good and necessary, and workers' freedom of action branded evil and selfish. We can conclude that the concept of negative freedom is essentially a class concept. It must now be clear that, to protect the fabric of the nation and the majority of the population from harm, we must restrict the freedom of people to engage in activities that cause this damage; in other words, they must be regulated. I speak of social reality rather than philosophical speculation.

Successive governments in the United Kingdom

have brought our political and economic system into crisis by their continued emphasis on the concept of negative freedom, presenting it as an absolute and a moral imperative. This emphasis is not essentially inherent to the concept of negative freedom, but that is how it is being utilised by the dominant ideology in modern society and, more particularly, the dominant neo-liberal political and economic ideology in the UK. This interpretation effectively negates the concept of positive freedom, and has produced damaging and divisive public policy, entrenched selfishness and greed in British culture, deeply damaged the normative order, and been dangerously exclusionary, serving narrow sectional interests at the expense of the greater population. As we noted earlier, its exclusionary policies have led to quite serious rioting in major UK cities and is in the process of dismantling the central institutions of British society and culture. Philosophical thinking may be abstract, but it does have real consequences, which often manifest themselves in public policy and legislation. Let me be clear, the concept of negative freedom is indeed very important, and should be cherished, but a one-sided approach to negative freedom adopted by neo-liberals is corrupting, as is everything neo-liberalism touches. The essential point is that the concept of freedom must not be taken as a given, as a "truth" or an "absolute". Negative freedoms, such as freedom of speech, assembly, religion and movement, are necessary for all human beings, but within the context of humanity's social nature. They cannot operate without the consideration of the need for other forms of freedoms as well.

Thomas Hobbes was the first political theorist to explicitly describe the concept of negative freedom. From a political perspective, negative freedom is a reaction and a response to the growth of the modern state and its increasing influence on our lives and behaviour. As a result, negative freedom is normally associated with the concept that we are free to the degree that we are not constrained by law or regulation, to the extent that we are able to do what we want, unhindered by external forces. This is the first pointer to the modern neo-liberal obsession with deregulation. As Isaiah Berlin describes it:

> I am normally said to be free to the degree to which no human being interferes with my activity. Political liberty in this sense is simply the area within which a man can act unobstructed by others. If I am prevented by other persons from doing what I could otherwise do, I am to that degree unfree; and if this area is contracted by other men beyond a certain minimum, I can be described as being coerced, or, it may be, enslaved.

It is important at this point to highlight that Berlin qualifies his concept of negative freedom by acknowledging the social nature of the human and noting that social life is interactive and interdependent, meaning that we are rarely able to act unobstructed by others. In that sense he does not condemn all restrictions on our activities as evil or wrong. The definitive discussion of freedom in the modern era is considered to be his essay that expanded on a lecture he delivered in Oxford University in 1958. Both the lecture and the essay were entitled "Two Concepts of Liberty" (the essay is the source of the above quote). The two different concepts under discussion were the concepts of negative and positive freedom. He begins his essay by explaining that he considers the words freedom and liberty to mean the same thing, and states that the concept of negative freedom is involved in the answer to the question, "What is the area within which the subject – a person or group of persons – is or should be left to do or be what he is able to do or be, without interference by other persons?" Positive freedom is involved in the answer to the question, "What, or who, is the source of control or interference, that can determine someone to do, or be, one thing rather than another?" The central theme of Berlin's argument is that, in his opinion, the concept of positive freedom has been used historically to control and repress individuals in the name of liberty.

Bertrand Russell in the preface to his 1947 edition of *A History of Western Philosophy* writes:

> I have tried ... to exhibit each philosopher, as far as truth permits, as an outcome of his milieu, a

man in whom were crystallised and concentrated thoughts and feelings which, in a vague and diffused form, were common to the community of which he was a part.

In other words, Russell recognises that each philosopher must be studied, in part, with regards to the environment, the situation and location, that he/she lived in. Each philosopher's thoughts and feelings are common to, and emanate from, his/her community. As a result, the philosopher is an individual, indeed in many ways a unique individual, but an individual who is to a greater or lesser extent a product of his/her environment. That is, his/her individuality cannot be understood without consideration of that environment. This is a definition of social being and an acceptance that a philosophy is an expression of collective social living. Each person is a social being, and individuality is a reflection of that social being. Of course each human who ever lived is an individual, but of necessity that individuality is a social individuality. It was Marx who said that the isolated individual human is a fiction. He writes, "The individual ... is the social being. ... Individual human life and species life are not different things" (*Economic and Philosophic Manuscripts of 1844*).

As a result, philosophers such as Hobbes, Bentham and Berlin are social beings and products of their environment, and their respective political philosophies will reflect that. I would argue that with respect to the concept of positive freedom, Berlin was asking the wrong question. If we apply Russell's methodology of exhibiting each philosopher as an outcome of their milieu, then Berlin's perception of positive freedom is most certainly from the viewpoint of particular bourgeois values; his milieu is betrayed as a class milieu. In support of that accusation, it should be noted that Berlin wrote in 1969 in his *Four Essays on Liberty* that "the essence of men is that they are autonomous beings – authors of values, of ends in themselves". Hopefully the reader will now acknowledge that statement to be simply wrong. Rather than seeing the human as an autonomous being and an author of values, we should be far more aware of how we are governed by our affective interests and our emotional impulses. As Sigmund Freud reminds us:

> Students of human nature and philosophers have long taught us that we are mistaken in regarding our intelligence as an independent force and in overlooking its dependence on emotional life. Our intellect, they teach us, can function reliably only when it is removed from the influences of strong emotional impulses; otherwise it behaves merely as an instrument of the will and delivers the inference which the will requires. Thus, in their view, logical arguments are impotent against affective interests, and that is why disputes backed by reasons... produce so few victories in the conflict with interests. Psycho-analytic experience has, if possible,

> further confirmed this statement. It can show every day that the shrewdest people will all of a sudden behave without insight, like imbeciles, as soon as the necessary insight is confronted by an emotional resistance, but that they will completely regain their understanding once that resistance has been overcome.
>
> *Sigmund Freud, Thoughts for the Times on War and Death (1915)*

According to Freud, we are mistaken if we regard our intelligence as being an independent force. In addition, we must also recognise, as David Hume says, that our reason is the slave of our passions, and that our passions (and our affective interests) are formed by our socialisation (that the essence of the human being is social is confirmed by Berlin's persistent reference to men, which is revealing of his middle-class, sexist approach). Yes, humans are the authors of values, but values are communal beliefs; they are not the gift of autonomous individuals. As we noted earlier, the human being needs other human beings in order to survive, before any considerations of individual needs or thoughts. Before we develop the capacity to speak, walk or feed ourselves, we are utterly dependent on other humans. As a result, our consciousness begins to develop in that milieu, in an environment of dependency on, and interaction with, other people. In other words, our consciousness is socially developed long before it is individually developed. Human beings are therefore capable of autonomy only to the extent that they act in accordance with, and are conscious of, the norms and values they have acquired in the process of socialisation – a process that predates any form of individual consciousness. This applies to the philosopher as much as to anyone else. You may argue that we are capable of applying criticism and reason to our own philosophies, but why would you question your own norms and values if not through human interaction: someone or something external to you that challenges you; some other person or human agent – a book, a radio or television report, or some social event like a riot or a war making you think and question your assumptions? You may argue that through the process of education and self-examination we can overcome our primary socialisation and embrace new and quite different attitudes and beliefs. This is true, but the process of education is itself highly social, and we are learning from people who are themselves a product of their milieu. So we can learn, we can develop intellectually, we can divorce ourselves from our old values, ideas and prejudices and embrace a completely different set of values and beliefs, but all of that is achieved within the social milieu of our environment, our social location. Yes, we can perform as an autonomous being, but our autonomy is qualified, it is not absolute, it is relative, it is a social production. As the French sociologist Auguste

Comte said, "The only absolute is that everything is relative!" And no, human beings are not an end in themselves; they are inexorably and essentially interdependent and interactive with other human beings. As Marx notes, our species being is a social being. Only someone from a classical liberal background would ask the question, "What, or who, is the source of control or interference, that can determine someone to do, or be, one thing rather than another?" Those who embrace the philosophy of individualism cannot conceptualise the collectivist empirical reality that most of the whats and whos that are the source of control or interference that Berlin is so concerned with are the norms and values that govern our behavior, that develop and exist within the society we are a product of and that we internalise in the process of our socialisation.

Organic forms of regulation develop in any society, some of them in the shape of formal law, but the vast majority as they emerge in the course of human social life – some indeed restrictive of our freedom but others that will enhance it. For Berlin such "whats" or "whos" that are the source of control or interference over us are essentially external to us, they are external constraints, whereas in reality, they are actually mostly internal, they are the norms and values and morals we have internalised in the course of our social and intellectual development, they are developed in the process of our socialisation.

By placing the concept of positive freedom within the framework of his question, "What, or who, is the source of control or interference, that can determine someone to do, or be, one thing rather than another?" Berlin is promoting the egoistic impulse onto a higher moral plane than the altruistic, just as Ayn Rand does with her Objectivist philosophy. Promoting altruistic values is therefore presented as repressive, as these values stifle the egoistic impulse, and this viewpoint is considered and presented as the "natural" position. This approach completely ignores the reality that the human being is often required to choose between egoism and altruism, between selfishness and sacrifice. Both are legitimate manifestations of individuality. There is nothing inherently "wrong" or "right" about either egoistic or altruistic choices, but the argument that positive freedom is ultimately repressive is the result of an individualist philosophy as opposed to a social philosophy, and is neither neutral nor moral.

Translated into the reality of modern Britain, advocates of negative freedom argue that government should leave as much activity to the market as possible. This includes social rights such as health and education. They require minimal government and a minimal state, and do not want the government to raise taxes to fund such things as this supposedly reduces their freedoms. They argue that people should have the freedom to spend their own money as they see fit, and not have to give it to the government in the form of taxation to pay for things that they may not agree with. This argument has a superficial plausibility, but in a money economy it is neither viable nor defensible. People who argue for negative freedom are quite prepared to pay taxes to fund the police and the armed forces, but go on to argue that most other aspects of society should be left to individual choice. In a money economy, such choices are only open to you if you have considerable financial resources. If you are unemployed or lack financial means in a capitalist money economy with privatised health and education you will end up illiterate, innumerate and, as your health suffers, dead! The counterargument provided by the neo-liberal Sir Keith Joseph, Social Security Minister in Mrs Thatcher's first government, was that "poverty is not unfreedom." Of course, each of us is perfectly free to starve, to die and to remain uneducated. It is repressive to take people's money in the form of taxation to pay for health care and education; indeed for thinkers such as Rand, Bentham and Keith Joseph, it is positively evil. For those of us who also believe in positive rights, denying people health care and education is not liberty; it is barbaric, the epitome of a selfish and morally bankrupt society!

Before discussing positive freedom in detail, I must qualify Berlin's argument, as his interpretation is not identical to the modern neo-liberal one. Berlin does accept that the freedom of some must

Freedom and Rights

be curtailed to secure the freedom of others and he asks the question: "upon what principle should this be done?" This demonstrates that he also accepts that freedom is not a moral absolute: if we consider it to be a sacred and untouchable value, there can be no principle on which we can curtail freedom for anyone. He concedes that we must be prepared to curtail freedom for reasons that cannot always be clearly stated or generalised into rules or universal maxims. For Berlin, the real debate centres on the area of control: how far does the government interfere with me? He concedes that freedom cannot be unlimited as that would lead to social chaos, and freedom must be curtailed in the cause of freedom itself, otherwise "people's minimum needs would not be satisfied and the liberties of the weak would be suppressed by the strong." On the area of control, he makes a distinction between private life and public authority, and then admits that it is possible, and indeed in some cases justifiable, to coerce people in the pursuit of social goals such as justice and public health, which they would agree to themselves if they were not "blind, or ignorant or corrupt". But he is still missing a crucial piece of the jigsaw: he insists that such actions by the authorities are necessarily coercive. It never seems to occur to the liberal individualist that people may have an egoistic self-interest in paying taxes for things like health care and education for other people as well as for themselves. Employers need healthy and educated workers for a successful business and it is in their self-interest to pay taxes for the state to provide that health and education rather than having to shoulder the whole burden themselves. By paying such taxes, they will make a larger profit, and, if people do exhibit such self-interest, then those mechanisms employed by the state in the interests of the employer (as well as the general population) cannot be described as coercive. They may well be in practice, or they may become coercive, but the point we must again stress is that this is neither necessarily, nor essentially, the case; they may indeed serve multiple interests that the neo-liberal considers to be mutually exclusive. However, Berlin then goes on to argue, quite correctly, that too often, people in authority use mechanisms such as taxation to justify coercive state measures on the grounds that they know what is good for "the people" better than the people themselves. What he fails to understand is that this is not restricted to those who pursue positive freedom, nor is it exclusive to societies who promote positive freedoms such as the Soviet Union and other communist-type states, or welfare states such as we had in the United Kingdom. The whole neo-liberal experiment in the UK since Thatcher has been based on the notion that the elite know what is best for all of us. Indeed it appears to be a universal characteristic of modern politicians. In reality, the centralisation that characterised communist societies has been increasing in our so-called liberal democracies for many years. Thus, in common with communist parties of the past, everything our modern so-called democratic politicians do is "the right thing to do".

Berlin goes on to show how, once this attitude is embraced, the authorities are:

> in a position to ignore the actual wishes of men or societies, to bully, oppress, torture them in the name, and on behalf, of their "real" selves, in the secure knowledge that whatever is the true goal of man (happiness, fulfilment of duty, wisdom, a just society, self-fulfilment) must be identical with his freedom – the free choice of his "true", albeit submerged and inarticulate, self.

Again when we consider the philosopher from the location of his milieu, the United Kingdom at the time Berlin was writing was a very different political and social system from what we see in the early twenty-first century. In modern neoliberal Britain, this willingness of the political elite to ignore the actual wishes of men or societies has been the justification for the invasion of nation states, dismantling the welfare state and the public sector, and the deregulation of large sectors of society.

Yes, socialist societies have been responsible for taking decisions without reference to those affected, but so have so-called liberal democracies. The notion that government and politicians know what is in my best interests better than I do myself is the last refuge of every scoundrel, regardless of political affiliation. It is also the antithesis of democracy.

Positive Freedom

In contrast with Sir Keith Joseph, the British liberal philosopher T.H. Green argued (1911) in favour of the concept of positive freedom, asserting that anyone prevented from realising their full potential was in a real sense unfree. Green argued that freedom was the ability of people to "make the best and most of themselves" and if they were not able to do this, then they were not free. Freedom to do, freedom from constraint, may look good in theory, but it is meaningless to those who lack the capacity to do what it is they wish to. As Green argued, freedom, to be meaningful, must involve real opportunities, not just theoretical ones. It is one thing to argue that all doors are open to us, it is quite another to be able to access them. As I have already argued, modern Britain, dominated by free market liberalism, is an exclusionary society and becoming more so each day. In theory the doors may be freely open and accessible, but government policy is increasingly ensuring that this remains just theory. The practical reality is that more and more people are being excluded and turned away before they can go through the doors. This is blindingly obvious in health and education policy making. The concept of positive freedom requires that individuals and social groups must be empowered before they can even begin to realise their potential. Until they can genuinely choose between options, they are not truly free. By only emphasising the value of negative freedom, as Berlin rightly points out, you simply erect a society in which the strong are in a position to freely exploit the weak.

As a result, regulatory measures must be taken to ensure that the strong are restrained and the weak empowered. This does not rob the stronger elements of society of their freedoms; it simply restricts total freedom, which is not a desirable social goal in the first place, as freedom is not an infinite resource, and as Lord Bingham pointed out, its limitation is necessary for the proper functioning of the rule of law. To repeat, one person's exercise of freedom is normally restrictive of another's. This requires active intervention in political and economic affairs, it requires regulation. It is a form of redistribution, in this case redistribution of opportunity. Any society that restricts potential academic brilliance from flourishing because potential students lack economic resources to access education deprives the wider society of talent and is, quite simply, stupid. A society that allows poor people to die because they're unable to purchase good health care – now that surely is an evil worthy of the name. I am not restricting your freedom by instituting taxation to pay for health and education: you will be able to access it as well. What I am restricting is your privilege, your ability to jump the queue, to exploit your social and economic position at the expense of the majority. It is no use trying to present this as implementing equality by coercive means, as all elitists try to do. It is not attempting to destroy the market system and replace it with "socialism". It is not seeking equality or an egalitarian society; it is seeking more equity, which is quite a different thing. It is in the pursuit of justice, fairness, and a less partial society. It is arguing for a society that will open opportunities for everyone and implement protections for the poor, the sick, the worker, for everyone's health and safety. An active interventionist state can be evil, but it can be beneficial as well. It all depends on the personnel charged with its administration. It can be argued, and has repeatedly been argued, that this is what the market seeks to achieve, and that it is only through market mechanisms that such goals can be realised. But this is demonstrably wrong, and is so on a worldwide scale, not only in the UK. It has been tried and has failed miserably. We have the empirical evidence that the market cannot and will not achieve such goals. That is what we mean when we state that the free market is a methodology, but a very poor methodology that can never achieve its aims. Its fundamental hypotheses are wrong and so its outcomes are wrong. Employers and political advocates of negative freedom argue that they must have the right to manage their business as they see fit. That however is a totally different thing from being allowed to do exactly as you please. The social interactive nature of the human being does not allow anyone to do exactly as they please. Thus, positive freedom requires positive intervention by government and the state, as indeed does negative freedom. Your negative freedoms must be protected where they do not infringe on, and do harm to, other human beings. Thus the state must take positive measures to protect our negative freedoms. Ironically, Berlin sums up the dangers of unregulated freedom by stating that "Freedom for the pike is death for the minnows." What is happening in modern Britain is that only the pike is allowed freedom, and the pikes are indeed using that freedom to bring about the death of the minnows.

Rights

This brings us to the consideration of rights, which again are defined in terms of positive and negative. In terms of negative rights there are many noble examples of historically defined negative rights that are granted to us by the simple fact of being human. For example, the American Declaration of Independence (1776) begins with the famous observation:

> We hold these truths to be self-evident, that all men are created equal, that they are endowed by their Creator with certain inalienable rights, that among these are Life, Liberty and the pursuit of Happiness. That to secure these rights, governments are instituted among men, deriving their just powers from the consent of the governed.

Whilst the French Declaration of the Rights of Man and Citizens (1789) states that:

Men are born free and equal in rights...the aim of every political association is the preservation of the natural and undoubted rights of men. These rights are liberty, property, security and resistance to oppression.

And the United Nations Universal Declaration of Human Rights (1948) states that:

> All human beings are born free and equal in dignity and rights. They are endowed with reason and conscience and should act toward one another in a spirit of brotherhood. ... The inherent dignity and the equal and inalienable rights of all members of the human family is the foundation of freedom, justice and peace in the world. Accordingly, all human beings regardless of race, colour, sex, language, religion, political or other opinion, national or social origin, property, birth or other status are entitled to those freedoms laid down in the Declaration.

As a result, such human rights are "universal" in the sense that they belong to all human beings irrespective of race, gender, sexual orientation, religion, the nation state they belong to or any other human social group. To deny people their human rights is to deny their humanity, and that is one of the charges against modern governments who seek to deny human rights in their so-called wars against terror. Such negative rights are under attack as never before in the UK on the pretext of protecting us from terrorist attack. The definition of terror is, however, being recast daily to deny the human rights of more and more citizens within society who are simply attempting to protest, quite legitimately and lawfully, and to challenge government and its policies. It is even being recast to include twelve-year-old children. The rights of protest, speech, assembly and movement are being eroded to protect an increasingly unaccountable and corrupt governing elite. As our rights are eroded, so too is our freedom, and that is why I argued earlier that the concept of negative freedom is to be cherished and protected. It is not negative freedom we criticise, but the nature of its interpretation and implementation. Thus, in the name of "freedom" our rights are being eroded and groups of people – Muslims, the poor, the disabled, people on benefits, the trades unions and working people in general – are being increasingly demonised and "dehumanised".

The distinction between freedom and rights is an artificial one, as freedom without rights is meaningless, and rights without freedom are similarly meaningless. Statements on human rights, such as we have just described, are agreed standards that must exist within nation states if the citizens are to be considered free. They are also the standards by which governments must design their policies in a free society. Thus, our political institutions have guidelines on how to secure and maintain our freedoms and rights. This is the essence of derivative and representative government. The purpose of government, according to the American Declaration of Independence, is "to secure these rights", and the purpose of government according to the French Declaration of the Rights of Man and Citizens is "the preservation of the natural and undoubted rights of men". If we return to Berlin's concept of the area of control that is central to his argument, then these basic human rights are the boundary of a government's area of control. They are called negative rights because they must never be legally or morally negated: that should be beyond government control. They are the boundary limits of legitimate governmental activity. The rights generally agreed to be covered by such statements of rights and freedom are freedom of speech, freedom of thought and religious belief, freedom from arbitrary arrest, freedom of association and assembly, freedom of movement, freedom of privacy, and equality before the law. These "negative" rights are those rights which are described in the Declarations as "natural" and "inalienable".

Positive rights are also known as legal rights and are those rights and freedoms we have been positively granted by law and other legal measures. They are normally legal expressions of our natural rights, and have been codified and formalised by the political system. For example, society erects positive limits on our rights to freedom of speech by protecting other people from libel, slander and racial harassment. Our right to freedom of speech is curtailed to protect other people's freedom from fear and intimidation. Therefore, positive rights have been established by society to ensure the protection of negative rights; they have been positively granted to the citizens of the state. Neo-liberal bourgeois individualists are only concerned with their own negative rights; they are completely unconcerned about other peoples. The paradox of positive and negative rights is something neo-liberals cannot understand: some of our negative rights must be curtailed to ensure other people's freedom and the preservation of their rights. Neo-liberal individualists believe their rights to be absolute, but freedom and rights must never be seen as absolutes, like everything else they are relative. Your freedom of speech ends when you use it to encourage hatred, discrimination and violence against me. Of course, some of these positive actions by any state may go too far. That is why political life is a process of trial and error. We may get the balance wrong and genuinely erect oppressive measures that do indeed curtail people's freedoms unnecessarily and, as a result, be forced to reflect and redress the balance. But that does not make positive freedom and rights inherently and essentially oppressive as the neo-liberal argues. Berlin conceded that point. Positive law and rights are human artefacts and, like everything else human, are subject to error and flaw, but that does not make them wrong, nor does it make everything we do in those areas wrong either. The classical liberal concept of government action as necessarily evil is simply wrong, and, as I continually stress, everything is relative. We should acknowledge that positive, or legal, rights are relative to each member of their respective society. They derive from, and exist in, particular countries and societies, and derive from our membership of that society, rather than from the simple fact that we are human. They will necessarily vary from country to country and reflect the laws and culture of each society. For example, in Britain some of the major examples of such measures enshrined in law are:

>Magna Charta 1215
>The Declaration of Arbroath 1320
>Habeas Corpus 1679
>The Bill of Rights 1689
>Catholic Emancipation Act 1829
>Abolition of Slavery 1833
>Sex Discrimination Acts 1975 and 1987
>Race Relations Act 1976

It should be noted that each of those measures that seek to enhance the freedom of large numbers of people, necessarily restrict and curtail the freedoms of others. If you perceive such measures as evil, I do not share the same moral language as you do.

As the British political structure is primarily based on parliamentary sovereignty along with an unwritten constitution, many of our rights stem from custom and practice, and thus are only protected by trust – that is, trust in the government to respect them. The principle of parliamentary sovereignty allows government to change, alter or abolish any and all of our rights whenever they see fit. The only hindrance to this power is our membership of the European Union and the vigilance of the Court of Human Rights, as some of their historic measures are the few sources left that are at least attempting to protect our human and employment rights. The particular nature of British politics means that our rights and freedoms are actually very fragile and can be removed with little difficulty. Since 1979, such rights have been under constant attack and continue to be eroded and diluted. Among the worst examples of this are employment rights, and the rights of protection from arbitrary stop and search treatment from the police.

Applying the notion of first principles, governments are derivative and therefore must be accountable to the people who elect them, pay their wages and invest them with the administrative authority by which they govern. This also means that their authority depends on the people respecting and sustaining that authority, and that they can forfeit and lose their authority and be dismissed by the people. In the context of British politics, no government is elected by the people. In Britain, we elect a parliament and the government is drawn from the members of that parliament. In other words, the government is indirectly elected. All members of the government are elected as constituency members of parliament, not as members of a government. When we elect our parliament, we know that the leader of the majority party will be Prime Minister, but that is all we know. However, that itself is merely a convention; there is no law that states that the leader of the majority party will become Prime Minister, and again, we are dependent on trust that this is what will occur following an election. Once elected that party leader will then proceed to form a government, and can make and unmake all members of the government during its term in office as he or she sees fit. During the term of a government its members can be quite numerous as people come and go as government ministers. In addition, the Prime Minister can change and the party can appoint a new Prime Minister, different from the person the people expected at the time of the election. This group of people can be appointed and dismissed on a whim, but whilst in office they hold our rights and freedoms in their hands and can do with them as they wish. The political norm within the UK is that all governments are elected on a minority of votes under the first-past-the-post electoral system. In other words, the British people need to watch and monitor governments like hawks. They must not be trusted. A good example was the governments of Tony Blair, whose legislative programme whilst in office was described by the British Law Lords as "the stuff of nightmares". A very telling remark by Prime Minister Blair was that our security is more important than our civil liberties. Indeed, one of his Home Office Ministers stated that Muslims in

Britain would have to accept the reality that they would be disproportionately targeted by the police in stop and search measures. If the politicians decide we warrant it, not only are we all going to be deprived of much of our liberty, but some groups in society are going to lose more than others. It could be argued that this particular approach amounts to the institutionalisation of racism and religious discrimination. We should be questioning whether it is possible to achieve any kind of security through the erosion of our civil liberties – surely a contradiction in terms. When we consider first principles, we are considering the basic concepts on which political theory and practice rest, and the justification, roles and functions of government and the state. Many commentators are concerned that the UK is developing into a form of police state and, if we allow this control to be imposed by a ruling elite that uses violence, coercion and constant surveillance, if the sovereign power of the nation does not reside within the people, if that sovereign power is unaccountable to the people or their elected parliament, or if the elected parliament meekly submits to an unaccountable government and administrative state and refuses to represent the will of the people who elected it, then authority is replaced by raw and unaccountable power, and the concept of justice becomes meaningless. In such a situation, liberty disappears, rights disappear or lose any significance and the democratic state is destroyed from within far more effectively than by a terrorist bomb. That is where the neo-liberals' interpretation of negative freedom and their attack on positive freedom is leading us!

Democracy requires a sovereign power, it is true. But for democracy to survive and flourish, this sovereign power must ensure that individual and collective rights are not imperilled. Remember, the several declarations of rights and freedom we looked at all stated that the protection of our rights and freedoms is the principal purpose of a democratic sovereign power. It must never be forgotten that the state and the government are social artefacts and are derivative from our human social nature. Their laws are also social artefacts, and therefore something is not good or moral simply because it is declared to be legal and something is not bad or immoral because it is illegal. Law merely reflects the dominant ideology in any given social situation. If something is "wrong" either morally or ethically, then making it legal does not make it right. Thus making it legal to deprive people of their liberty without due process of law, or without even telling people why they are being deprived of their liberty, will never make it "right" under the fundamental first principles of a free society. The treatment of people like the Libyan lady Ms Bouchar can never be justified. No government has any right to sanction and defend such behaviour, and no officer of the state can be excused for carrying out such behaviour, whether it is officially sanctioned or not. Nor, despite all the assurances of our political class, will it make anyone in the society, including the elite, secure. The American Declaration of Independence states that it is self-evident that all men are created equal, and endowed by their Creator with certain inalienable rights, that among these are life and liberty, and it is to secure these rights that governments are instituted amongst men, deriving their powers from the consent of the governed. If it is self-evident that the state is charged with upholding the life and liberty of its citizens, then no government can justify dismantling the mechanisms erected in the state for the preservation of these inalienable rights. In addition, how much power should you be entitled to derive from twenty-five per cent of the electorate – the normal electoral mandate gained by British governments? Whilst Tony Blair was telling us that our security was more important than our liberties, he was representing a government whose party was elected in 2001 with only 24 out of every hundred voters and in 2005 with only 22 out of every hundred voters. In 2001 there was a voter turnout of 59% that gave Labour a majority of 166 seats with 40.7% of the votes cast and in 2005 Labour gained a 65 seat majority with 35.2% of a 61.4% turnout. That gave Labour 24.2% of all possible votes in 2001 and 21.6% in 2005 (House of Commons Library). Are those levels of popular support of possible votes enough to justify depriving one hundred per cent of the people of their basic inalienable rights? As citizens and electors of the British state, we are entitled to ask, and to receive answers to all such questions. Especially from a head of government who is not directly elected. The Declaration of Independence goes on to warn that whenever any form of government becomes destructive of these ends, that is the securing of life and liberty, then it is the right of the people to alter or abolish that form of government. These are first principles, not only of the American system of government, but of all other governments. If our security is more important than our civil liberties, then what does it matter who governs us? What is it governments seek to secure anyway, if it is not our liberty and rights? Without our rights and liberties what kind of secure life will we have? Would we be any more secure in such a state than the Germans were under Hitler or the Russians under Stalin? Blair's argument is as stupid as it is false. It is also quite sinister!

If we do not accept that governments have either the right or authority to dilute or remove our fundamental rights and inflict torture, we must address one of the most commonly used justifications of torture and suspension of human rights by nations such as the United Kingdom. Time and again politicians ask the rhetorical question: what should we do if we know someone has information about a forthcoming terrorist atrocity in our cities and streets which could cause thousands of casualties? They argue that the only way to prevent this catastrophe is to gain the information by methods that are classified as torture. The first point is that, in all the years since we embarked on our so-called war on terror, such a circumstance has never arisen. This scenario is repeatedly raised by our politicians and security services despite the fact that they have not as yet had to confront it. As a result, it is being embedded in the nation's consciousness that such things are indeed a real possibility. The purpose of this scaremongering is to secure the consent of the people to commit atrocities against other human beings whether or not there is a real motive for it, and to justify the torture of people who have been arrested by the United States and Britain without any concrete evidence to support their suspicions. One of the biggest lies perpetrated by our authorities is that if we have nothing to hide, then we have nothing to worry about. That again is demonstrable nonsense; we all have cause to worry about the activities of our authorities, and none of us know when it will be our turn. A young Brazilian man, Jean Charles de Menezes was shot to death by the police in a public place in London for absolutely no reason. It could therefore happen to anyone. All of us have things we don't want other people to know about, and again, such things are no business of our politicians or security services. The next point to make is that the demonstrable mendacity of our political leaders, coupled with the incompetence and undoubted mendacity of the security services and the police should make us very careful about what we believe from these sources. We are always being assured that "the authorities" have thwarted plots and uncovered conspiracies to launch terrorist atrocities against our nation, and we are expected to simply accept such assurances with no proof. Perhaps they are indeed authentic, but we should know the circumstances and never have to accept the word of proven liars (remember we had a Prime Minister who convinced Parliament and the nation that we had to launch a full-scale invasion of the sovereign state of Iraq because it was "beyond doubt" that Iraq possessed weapons of mass destruction, and was fully supported by one of the most senior law officers in the UK, the Attorney General – a legal officer who was quite aware that Parliament and the people were being comprehensively lied to in his name). As a result of such supposed plots and conspiracies, we are continually being urged to accept increasing dilution of our rights and freedoms in the name of this illusion of security. By the same process of fraud and deception, the police get more powers, rights are eroded, cameras and surveillance equipment proliferate in our towns and cities, our phones are tapped and the government demands the right to monitor every email and text sent by everyone in the United Kingdom. All this is, of course, for our own good, and it is purely coincidental that it is also extremely lucrative business for the security industry, members of which pay large sums of money to our political parties.

However, even if there was evidence in some cases, none of that applied in the cases we discussed above, those of Binyam Mohamed, Shaker Aamer or Ms Bouchar. These people were arrested and tortured for no other reason than that they were the victims of gross incompetence by the intelligence services, the same services that assured us of Iraq's weapons of mass destruction. It was enough that they were Muslims, and, on that basis, they were tortured, stripped of their human rights and subjected to appalling treatment from both our security services and our government. How such behaviour is designed to protect our security is a mystery to anyone. What it does is breed towering resentment and hostility throughout the Islamic nations and give credence to extremist propaganda. There is a legitimate debate to be had in the UK on the question of our security and the measures governments have embraced, and our human rights. The emphasis has been at the expense of our human rights and our real long-term security. The threat to our security and rights comes, not from foreign forces and governments, not from extremist elements in the Muslim world, but from the extremists within our neo-liberal elite, from forces within the very establishment of the UK itself. All the measures taken in the name of the so-called war on terror are, in reality, designed to further the agenda and policies of neo-liberal economics. The war on terror is designed to facilitate the worldwide ambitions of economic hegemony by extreme free-marketeers. It is time our peoples woke up to the corrosive and corrupting influence of this ideological warfare that has the intention of removing all constraints on its activities, and all our rights that constrain such activities. For the neo-liberal, if that requires torture, then so be it!

Conclusion

In the Gospel According to St Matthew (7:15-16), Christ tells his disciples, "Beware of false prophets which come to you in sheep's clothing but inwardly they are ravening wolves / Ye shall know them by their fruits. Do men gather grapes of thorns or figs of thistles?" And in Matthew 7:19-20, he tells them, "Every tree that bringeth not forth good fruit is hewn down and cast into the fire / Wherefore by their fruits ye shall know them."

This is an instruction, reinforced by repetition, that in order to understand reality we must take an empirical approach. It is a warning that what people tell us is not nearly as important as what they do. This is excellent advice. If we want to know what people stand for, what their real agenda is, we learn not from what they claim to be or to represent, but by their actions and by their fruits. Christ admonishes us to be alert to the fact that what people say and what they then do can be very different things. The neo-liberal is the prototypical false prophet who comes to us in sheep's clothing, but is inwardly a ravening wolf. How do we know this? By his/her fruits! Since Margaret Thatcher took office, successive governments have assaulted our human rights in pursuit of economic imperatives and in doing so have seriously eroded the rule of law. They have attacked, diluted, or removed, every obstacle to the economic goals of the free market and the accumulation of unlimited and unregulated wealth that traditionally stood in the way of what they term "wealth creation". Many of these perceived obstacles were erected in Britain over many years for the protection of the weak and vulnerable from the worst excesses of "the market". As a result the clarion call of the free-marketeer is the "liberation" of the market. It is the contention of this work that the liberation of the market has resulted in the increasing enslavement and pauperisation of the rest of society. Liberty is not an unlimited resource, and bestowing liberty on some people, or groups of people, often means restricting others, and, in granting negative freedoms in the context of the neo-liberal agenda, has meant removing or diluting other people's positive freedoms and rights, those positive rights that enable people to be full participants in society, both politically and economically. Increasing liberty for neo-liberal interests has meant decreasing liberty for the rest of the population, with the result that their prosperity, quality of life, and life chances have been seriously eroded. British government has taken upon itself the protection of elite and class interests, and has shown itself to be quite prepared to abandon and subvert the rule of law, the normative order and Britain's traditional moral order in pursuit of neo-liberal goals and objectives. In doing so, it has subverted an entire value system and corrupted the institutions of the British state. I have argued that the state is not necessarily evil, but I am afraid that, under the direction of the neo-liberal, it has become so. This has resulted in a complete loss of trust in our traditional institutions – in government, the political class, the police, the legal system and the press. Throughout this process, the authorities have pursued an ideological programme that is both anti-social and ultimately self-destructive. This programme has failed but, in order to camouflage the fundamental causes of its failures, the authors of this programme have sought to scapegoat their failings. To successfully achieve this they have demonised large groups of people who are in fact the victims of a massive neo-liberal fraud, the poor, the unemployed, the sick, the disabled and the Muslim community. How have they got away with this crime? By holding the levers of power at all levels of society, particularly the levers of opinion-making, and they act together as a unified elite class. The biggest lie they peddle is the old saw that "we are all in it together." Oh no, we certainly aren't, but when it comes to perpetrating a fraud on the British public, the elite most certainly are in it together. Free market economics reduces everything to a commodity. Most commodities (and in the neo-liberal universe that includes rights, law and obligations) have a price, which is also a cost, but some commodities have no exchange value in the market and are only a cost. So, in market terms they have no value, they are useless. Someone who cannot work, for whatever reason, is useless and valueless; they are a cost, and costs must be minimised and if possible eliminated. The neo-liberal commodifies health, education, welfare and people. It commodifies rights; look for example at the neo-liberal war against health and safety. One of the fundamental rights we should enjoy is the right to a safe and secure workplace. But health and safety is a cost to the employer and so the neo-liberal rubbishes health and safety as unnecessary and burdensome. Other positive rights attacked by the neo-liberal as unnecessary and overburdening costs are pensions, holidays, overtime, holiday pay and night shift allowances. But the biggest targets of the neo-liberal are the benefits system and health, and the rights embedded within these institutions. The bodies which traditionally secured many of our workplace rights were the labour unions, and so an unceasing war of denigration and subversion is waged against the trade union movement, removing their gains, diluting their bargaining power, and in many cases removing their bargaining rights altogether. The unions are openly portrayed as the enemy of British society and as parasites. Thatcher publicly branded Britain's miners as "the enemy within", and every union member in the United Kingdom as a potential enemy spy, when she banned union membership in the Government's Communications Headquarters on the grounds that it compromised Britain's security. Unions and their members are not entitled to rights. The neo-liberals in government and the press have successfully generated a climate of hatred towards trades unions within British society, which reflects their hatred of working people. The only intrinsic value in the free market is economic, to the point that society has no values other than economic. The only "right" that matters and that must be protected, is the right to make profits and to accumulate wealth. People have no value in themselves outwith their capacity for production and use value in the "market". As a result, the unemployed, the disabled and the sick are all seen as costs and worthless other than as units of consumption, and they are not very valuable even then, as their purchasing power is minimal.

This explains the constant denigration of such groups by the neo-liberal elite and their lackeys in the media. This denigration and constant criticism has a desired end, the dehumanisation of such groups. Britain's ruling elite have purposely and deliberately bred hatred and contempt throughout society for the most vulnerable. The period since the start of the economic crisis in August 2007 has witnessed a dramatic and genuinely shocking rise in hate crimes against the disabled that is adequately documented in the press. As I have already remarked, neo-liberal Britain is an exclusionary society and the dehumanisation of the poor, sick and disabled is part of the process of exclusion. As a result, whole groups of people within modern Britain are being excluded from meaningful participation in society and effectively disenfranchised. The political system has no personnel in decision-making positions who have sympathy with such groups or any desire to represent them. Any such personnel that existed in the past has been systematically excluded. Very few of the decision-makers within our parliament and civil service have any life experience outside of the elite circles they have lived in throughout their lives. The political system has become hereditary to the extent that the political class operate a very exclusionary policy within their parties that sees advancement within the system being dependent on sharing the same background and views of the ruling elite. If you are not "one of us", then you are simply excluded, and this applies equally to all three major parties. Thatcher had already successfully marginalised organised labour, and the lessons learned from that process have been enthusiastically adopted in relation to other groups.

This process has, of course, a desired end, to deny such groups their fundamental rights. You need not bother with the human rights of those you have stripped of their humanity, what the Nazis called the *untermenschen*. *Untermenschen* translates as "underman", but is better understood as the Nazis interpretation of subhuman. The principal subhuman in Nazi ideology was of course the Jew. In modern Britain it is the Muslim, who is seen as following different loyalties that could undermine the modern British state. The Nazis had another extraordinary term for those people they considered useless, the *ballastexistenzen*. These people were "human ballast", who could be thrown overboard when the ship of state got into difficulties, and were actually described in Nazi literature as "useless eaters". They included the mentally ill and the physically handicapped, and were fit only for extermination, as they had no productive capacity and were an intolerable cost. Is it merely coincidence that Britain's neo-liberal government is subjecting the physically and mentally handicapped to "fit for work" tests? Or is it simply that neo-liberals perceive people who are not fit for work as useless eaters, consuming valuable resources that could more properly be utilised by other people who contribute to the economic well-being of the neo-liberal market? When I contemplate the government's policies on such matters the term *"Arbeit Macht Frei"* somehow springs to mind.

As a result, we have a society that actively seeks to create a free market in every area of life, and which cannot, and will not, tolerate constraints being placed on its activities. Human rights are a constraint, the rule of law is a constraint, positive freedoms and rights are constraints. One of the major goals of the free market is a free labour market. Each person who works, whether in a waged or a salaried position, has their worth calculated in monetary terms. People must be bought and sold within this labour market as commodities, whether they be dustmen or bankers. Their monetary value is, we are assured, determined by "the market" (which is clearly false). However, this monetary value is also the value that is placed on their "use value" to society, which is also the measure of their humanity and the extent that they should be included in that society, and if a person has no monetary value because they are incapable of entering the labour market, then they have no human value either as they contribute nothing to the society.

Fundamental to the argument of this book is the proposition that "the market" is an illusion that doesn't exist in the form that is presented to us by the theories and propositions that supposedly underpin it. The free market is a fraud that does not and cannot work and is a demonstrably empirical fraud whose foundations have been built on sand and a whole industry of lies. If you establish a normative order based on the perception that human beings are commodities to be bought, sold and exchanged, you create a ripple effect that you will have difficulty controlling. If you dehumanise the person to the extent that you view them as a "thing" to be used and discarded, hired and fired at will, then you dehumanise humanity itself, and, of course, human rights do not apply to the subhuman. Thus it is all right to torture Muslims and subject them to rendition, to completely immobilise a pregnant woman for seventeen hours and deny her any kind of sustenance, because after all, she's just a Muslim! It is all right to deny the working person the right to strike, as this interferes with the market and disrupts normal business, to strip them of their pension, their redundancy rights, their unfair dismissal rights, as these are all unjustifiable constraints on economic recovery. It is all right, under the government's own guidelines, to require someone who is terminally ill with cancer, but who has been given over six months to live, to actively seek a job or lose their benefits. To allow them to live out their remaining days preparing for an inevitable death in peace and dignity would be an intolerable burden on the long-suffering taxpayer. How dare these selfish bastards demand to be kept by the taxpayer for six months when they could be contributing to their own funeral costs in a meaningful way?

It is my conviction that the free market experiment begun by Thatcher has failed, that it has demonstrably failed, and that it is corrupting the whole of society. It has corrupted, and continues to corrupt, all the traditional institutions of British society. It is destroying the political system and is leading to the break-up of the United Kingdom. It is the cause of rioting and looting that will surely get worse, and has brought the fruits of terrorism onto our streets. The greed and rapacity of the British elite knows no limits and it refuses to exercise any form of self-restraint. Its members continually attempt to remove all constraints on their ability to loot the national treasury, constraints that include everyone else's rights and legal protections and the normative order that regulates social life. The future is not what it used to be! The fundamental concepts and theories that underpin the dominant ideology in modern Britain are simply wrong. They must be challenged and exposed as wrong! Free market economics and neo-liberal economic and political theory are not simply theory and ideology, they are the means to obtain ends. They are the methods employed to allow the theories to operate, to allow free market and neo-liberal goals to be realised. They are also flawed methods that ensure that the desired ends will never be met, but in the meantime they are also very destructive and dangerous. Despite what our noble elite tell us, there are alternatives, there are other choices. There are always choices. Human rights and the rule of law must never be subjected to the imperatives of the market and considered as either costs or constraints. Economics must never be allowed to subvert our rights and the rule of law, a rule that requires everything, including the market, to be subject to law, equally applicable to everyone. Remember, the law knows no favourites.